Financing College Tuition

Financing College Tuition

Government Policies and Educational Priorities

Marvin H. Kosters, editor

The AEI Press

Publisher for the American Enterprise Institute
WASHINGTON, D.C.

1999

Available in the United States from the AEI Press, c/o Publisher Resources Inc., 1224 Heil Quaker Blvd., P.O. Box 7001, La Vergne, TN 37086-7001. To order: 1-800-269-6267. Distributed outside the United States by arrangement with Eurospan, 3 Henrietta Street, London WC2E 8LU England.

Library of Congress Cataloging-in-Publication Data

Financing college tuition : government policies and educational
    priorities / Marvin H. Kosters, editor.
        p. cm.
    "Publisher for the American Enterprise Institute."
    Includes bibliographical references and index.
    ISBN 0-8447-4075-6 (cloth : alk. paper).—ISBN 0-8447-4076-4
(pbk. : alk. paper)
    1. Education, Higher—United States—Finance.   2. Education,
Higher—United States—Finance—Government policy.   3. Federal aid
to higher education—United States.   4. College costs—United
States.   I. Kosters, Marvin H.   II. American Enterprise Institute
for Public Policy Research.
LB2342.F495   1999
379.1'214'0973—dc21   99-38640
                                                                       CIP

1   3   5   7   9   10   8   6   4   2

THE AEI PRESS
Publisher for the American Enterprise Institute
1150 17th Street, N.W., Washington, D.C. 20036

Printed in the United States of America

Contents

CONTRIBUTORS   ix

1 INTRODUCTION   *Marvin H. Kosters*   1

2 BUDGETS, PRIORITIES, AND INVESTMENT IN HUMAN
CAPITAL   *Eric A. Hanushek*   8

3 WHERE SHOULD FEDERAL EDUCATION INITIATIVES BE
DIRECTED?   *Caroline M. Hoxby*   28

4 REFORMING PUBLIC SUBSIDIES FOR HIGHER
EDUCATION   *Thomas J. Kane*   53

5 CAN TUITION POLICY COMBAT RISING WAGE
INEQUALITY?   *Stephen V. Cameron and James J. Heckman*   76

TABLES

2–1   Public School Resources, 1961–1991   12
2–2   Population with Upper-Secondary-Level Education, by
Age and Country, 1992   16
3–1   Education-Related Appropriations and Tax Expenditures,
Fiscal Year 1998   29
3–2   Education-Related Appropriations and Tax Expenditures,
Fiscal Year 1999   30
3–3   Education-Related Appropriations and Tax Expenditures,
Budget for Fiscal Year 2000   31
3–4   Increasing Competitiveness of the U.S. Market for
Baccalaureate Education, 1949–1994   32
3–5   Effects of Competition on Elementary and Secondary
Schooling   40
4–1   Probability of Postsecondary Enrollment by State Tuition,
Need-Based Grant Spending, and Unemployment Rate for
the Class of 1982   62

4–2 Changes in College Enrollment Rates of Dependent
Eighteen- to Nineteen-Year-Old Females, by Family-
Income Quartile, 1970–1972 to 1973–1977   64
5–1 College Entry by Type of College First Attended for High
School Graduates and GED Recipients at Age Twenty-four   92
5–2 College Entry by Age Twenty-four for High School
Graduates and GED Holders by Type of College First
Attended and Quartile of the White Family-Income
Distribution   93
5–3 Mean Characteristics by Race Group   96
5–4 Changes in the White-Minority Schooling Gap with
Minority Variables Equated to White Levels   100
5–5 Effects of $10,000 Increase in Family Income on College
Entry of High School Graduates and GED Holders by Type
of College First Attended   109
5–6 Effects of $1,000 Increase in Gross Tuition on College-Entry
Probabilities of High School Graduates and GED Holders
by Family-Income Quartile and by AFQT Quartile   111
5–7 P-Values of Chi-Square Test of Equal Magnitude of $1,000
Rise in Tuition and $1,000 Rise in Family Income   113

FIGURES

2–1 Real Spending per Student, 1890–1990   11
2–2 International Test Score Performance, for Selected
Countries, 1963–1991   14
2–3 NAEP Mathematics Achievement Score for Seventeen-
Year-Olds, by Race or Ethnicity, 1973–1994   18
3–1 Market Competitiveness of K–12 and Higher Education,
1950–1990   33
3–2 Share of Revenues to K–12 Schools from Local Sources,
1950–1990   34
3–3 Federal Share of K–12 and Higher Education Revenues,
1960–1990   35
3–4 Use of Collective Bargaining and Teacher Organizations by
Public School Teachers, 1960–1990   36
3–5 Enrollment at Private K–12 and Higher Education Schools,
1960–1990   37
3–6 Growth of U.S. Net Exports of Higher Education,
1970–1995   42
4–1 College Enrollment Rates and College Wage Premiums,
1967–1995   54
4–2 Proportion of High School Classes of 1982 and 1992
Entering a Four-Year College, by Family Income   55

4–3   Projected Growth in Fifteen- to Twenty-four-Year-Old
      Population, 1995–2015   60

5–1   College Participation by Eighteen- to Twenty-four-Year-
      Old High School Graduates and GED Holders, 1970–1996   78

5–2   College-Entry Proportions of Twenty-one- to Twenty-four-
      Year-Old High School Graduates and GED Holders,
      1970–1996   79

5–3   Distribution of Schooling Attainment for Males at Age
      Fourteen and Age Twenty-four   85

INDEX   125

Contributors

STEPHEN V. CAMERON is an assistant professor of economics and public affairs at Columbia University. From 1991 to 1994 he was a research associate at the Harris School of Public Policy at the University of Chicago. Mr. Cameron's research interests include labor economics, human capital, applied econometrics, and applied microeconomics. He has had several articles published in professional journals, most recently in the *Journal of Political Economy* (1998) and the *Journal of Labor Economics*. In 1993, Mr. Cameron published "Comment on Trends in College Entry among Whites, Blacks, and Hispanics" in *Studies in the Supply and Demand of Higher Education.*

ERIC A. HANUSHEK is a professor of economics and public policy and the director of the W. Allen Wallis Institute of Political Economy at the University of Rochester. He joined the University of Rochester in 1978 and has been the director of its Public Policy Analysis Program and the chairman of the Department of Economics. From 1983 to 1985 he was the deputy director of the Congressional Budget Office. His research involves applied public finance and public policy analysis with special emphasis on educational issues. He has also investigated the determination of individual incomes and wages, housing policy, and the economics of discrimination. His publications include *Assessing Policies for Retirement Income, Improving America's Schools, Modern Political Economy, Making Schools Work, Educational Performance of the Poor, Improving Information for Social Policy Decisions,* and *Education and Race,* along with numerous articles in professional journals.

JAMES J. HECKMAN is the Henry Schultz Distinguished Service Professor at the University of Chicago. He is a senior fellow of the American Bar Foundation and the director of the Center for Social Program Evaluation at the University of Chicago. Mr. Heckman was a lecturer and an associate professor at Columbia University from 1970 to 1973 and a visiting professor at Yale from 1988 to 1990. He was a fellow of the Center for Advanced Study in the Behavioral Sciences at Stanford in 1978–1979. He is a member of the National Academy of Sciences and the American Academy of Arts and Sciences and a fellow of the Econometric Society. Mr. Heckman received the John Bates Clark Award in 1983.

He has written numerous articles on labor economics, the economics of discrimination, public sector economics and the economics of the bureaucracy, cost-benefit analysis, the evaluation of social programs, and econometrics. His monograph *The Economic Evaluation of Social Programs* is forthcoming.

CAROLINE MINTER HOXBY is an associate professor of economics at Harvard University, where she has been on the faculty since 1994. She is also a research fellow of the National Bureau of Economic Research. Ms. Hoxby's teaching and research are concerned with the economics of education, the labor market, and local governments. Her recent work on K–12 education includes papers on private school vouchers, private school choice, and choice among public schools. She has had numerous articles published in the *Quarterly Journal of Economics, American Economic Review,* and *Journal of Public Economics.* Ms. Hoxby has worked with several states on their constitutional school-finance court cases. Her current projects include a study of how market forces shape American colleges and universities.

THOMAS J. KANE is an associate professor of public policy at the Kennedy School of Government, Harvard University. Mr. Kane was the senior economist for labor, education, and welfare at the Council of Economic Advisers from 1995 to 1996, and he is currently a faculty research fellow at the National Bureau of Economic Research. He has also been a visiting fellow at the Brookings Institution. Mr. Kane's main research interests include labor economics, education policy, applied econometrics, and human services. He has had numerous articles published in the *National Tax Journal, Quarterly Journal of Economics, American Economic Review,* and *Journal of Political Economy.* Mr. Kane also wrote *The Price of Admission: Rethinking How Americans Pay for College* (Brookings, forthcoming).

MARVIN H. KOSTERS is a resident scholar and the director of economic policy studies at the American Enterprise Institute. He was a senior economist at the President's Council of Economic Advisers and at the White House Office of the Assistant to the President for Economic Affairs. Mr. Kosters also held a senior policy position at the U.S. Cost of Living Council and a research position at the RAND Corporation. He is the author of *Wage Levels and Inequality* (1998), the coeditor of *Trade and Wages: Leveling Wages Down?* (1994) and of *Reforming Regulation* (1980), and the editor of *The Effects of the Minimum Wage on Employment* (1996), *Personal Saving, Consumption, and Tax Policy* (1992), and *Workers and Their Wages* (1991). Mr. Kosters has contributed to *American Economic Review* and *The Public Interest.*

1
Introduction

Marvin H. Kosters

The education level of the American work force has been substantially upgraded during this century. High school credentials were becoming more common before World War II, and college attendance was increasing. In 1940, about half of the young people were completing high school, and about 5 percent graduated from college. Now, most young people either graduate from high school or receive an equivalency certificate. College credentials have likewise become increasingly common, especially among the generation that became adults during the 1970s and 1980s. The proportion of young adults with four years of college or more has ranged between 20 and 25 percent for the past twenty years.[1] The rising education level of the work force has contributed importantly to the growth of productivity and real incomes in the United States, and upgraded schooling levels have been one of the most important ways in which successive generations achieved higher living standards than their parents.

The pronounced increase in the proportion of the work force with college-level credentials in the 1970s temporarily reduced the relative wages of young college graduates. By the 1980s, however, the growing importance of college for attaining higher real earnings was becoming increasingly apparent. The differential between wages earned by workers with only high school credentials or less and wages earned by college graduates widened substantially. Moreover, the wider college–high school wage differential resulted in part from a decline in the level of real wages for workers with high school credentials or less. Under these circumstances, college seemed to provide the key to increases in real wages and living standards.

---

1. The percentages reported are for youths twenty-five to twenty-nine years old. Data starting from 1947 are taken from U.S. Bureau of the Census (1947, 96–97, t. 18). Fragmentary data to the beginning of the century on school enrollment and completion were reported by the President's Commission on Higher Education (1947).

The difficulty in paying for a college education that some young people and their parents experienced attracted increased attention as enrollment rose. The rise in the college wage premium encouraged more young people to enroll in postsecondary schooling, but college enrollment rose less quickly for youths from low-income families, and their enrollment rates remained well below enrollment for youths from families with higher incomes. Moreover, steep increases in tuition costs meant that out-of-pocket costs for attending college were rising more rapidly than family income and other prices. In this context proposals to help finance college tuition costs were enacted in 1997.[2]

New policies to provide additional money at the federal level for postsecondary schooling raise a number of questions: Is schooling at the college level most in need of national policy attention? Are problems at the elementary and secondary level more pressing? Will more resources be effective in ameliorating shortcomings in educational performance? What kinds of policies to improve education can best be carried out at the federal level? Will making more money available to pay college tuition and other costs increase college enrollment? Will assurance that grants, loans, and tax abatement will be available to help pay out-of-pocket costs for college appreciably reduce disparities in college enrollment for families with different income levels? If money is not the main problem, might it nevertheless be worthwhile to ease the financial costs of college for parents? This book's contributors evaluate the new policies to provide for additional federal financial support for college in essays that address these and other questions.

College Tax Credits: The Taxpayer Relief Act of 1997

When he began his second term in 1997, President William Clinton proposed an increase in federal support for education of about 50 percent. Most of the proposed increase was for postsecondary schooling, and most of that was devoted to tax relief. Providing additional financial support for college has considerable popular appeal, with enrollment in postsecondary schooling a realistic expectation for a majority of youths and the aspiration of many parents.

The goal of President Clinton's proposals for additional financial support for postsecondary schooling, as he stated in his February 1997

---

2. A National Commission on the Cost of Higher Education was established in August 1997, and the commission published its report in January 1998. Data presented in this report show larger increases in college tuition costs than in incomes, based on various measures presented there, but these data also show a slowdown in tuition cost escalation in the mid-1990s.

State of the Union message, was to "make the 13th and 14th years of education, at least 2 years of college, just as universal in America by the 21st century as a high school diploma is today" (President 1997). This goal echoed an earlier report of the President's Commission on Higher Education. In its discussion of the goals and the steps that need to be taken to achieve them, that report says, "The time has come to make education through the 14th grade available in the same way that high school is now available"—that is, without the need to pay tuition and fees. This latter statement comes from a presidential commission that issued its report about fifty years earlier, in 1947 (PCHE 1947).

The idea of making two years of college commonplace and available with little or no out-of-pocket costs is not new, but conditions were quite different when the commission's report was written. At that time, more than 40 percent of total college enrollment consisted of World War II veterans who were enrolled under the GI bill. About 28 percent of college-age youths (eighteen and nineteen years old) were enrolled in school then compared with more than 60 percent now. At that time, the United States had troops stationed in Germany and Japan as occupation forces. In two years the Soviet Union would set off its first atomic explosion. These circumstances provide some insight into the social, political, and security concerns that motivated the establishment of the commission.

The view that the out-of-pocket costs of college that are represented by tuition and other fees are a significant impediment to college enrollment for low-income youths has a long history. The Report of the Presidential Commission of 1947 says, for example, "Low family income, together with the rising costs of education, constitutes an almost impassible barrier to college education for many young people." The remedy for these circumstances that was proposed, then as now, was more financial assistance at the national level. The form of financial assistance recommended then—"a nationally financed system of scholarships and fellowships"—was in many ways more limited, however, than the system of need-based grants and loans and of tax credits that characterizes our current system for providing federal financial assistance for postsecondary schooling (PCHE 1947, vol. 1, 28, and vol. 5, 4).

The programs that were enacted in 1997 to help parents finance the costs of postsecondary schooling were different in many details, but not in their broad substance, from those initially proposed by the Clinton administration. The bulk of the additional federal support that was initially proposed (about $40 billion over five years) was to be almost evenly divided between a tax credit of $1,500 for up to two years and a tax deduction of up to $10,000 for two years. Almost

3

$2 billion of the proposed total was devoted to larger grants for college students from low-income families by increasing the limits for Pell grants. The basic approach was to make more money available to low-income families by increasing the maximum size of grants and to middle-income families by reducing their tax liabilities.

The component of the tax benefits that is applicable for the first two years of postsecondary schooling (the Hope tax credit) provides a dollar-for-dollar credit for the first $1,000 of a taxpayer's qualified out-of-pocket expenses and a 50 percent credit for the next $1,000, for a maximum of $1,500. Benefits under this credit are available for each student for only the first two years of postsecondary schooling. The tax benefits that are applicable beyond the first two years of postsecondary schooling (the lifetime learning credit) provide a tax credit for each taxpayer equal to 20 percent of the first $5,000 of qualified expenses until the year 2002, after which the limit rises to $10,000. The credits are phased out above prescribed income levels, and a student can benefit from only one of the credits in any year.

In addition to these programs of tax credits, a new type of individual retirement account was established and the tax penalty was removed for funds withdrawn from other IRAs to pay education expenses. The new education IRAs permit up to $500 per year to be deposited in such an account for children under eighteen, and gains for these accounts are not taxable when the proceeds are used for qualified expenditures for postsecondary education. For money used to pay such expenses that is withdrawn from other IRAs, however, gains are taxable, but the 10 percent penalty that would otherwise be applied below age 59.5 is eliminated. The individual income tax code was also modified to permit deduction of interest paid on student loans (under prescribed circumstances) (IRS 1997).

Overview

In public discussions of federal policies influencing education, different levels of education are almost always considered separately, in the context of specific programs that affect them. Thus, the importance of the early childhood experience is often emphasized for preschool programs; issues such as standard setting, school construction, and teacher training for elementary and secondary schooling; and financial assistance to help pay tuition and fees for postsecondary schooling. In higher education, for example, policy discussion is often concentrated on questions such as how much subsidy should be provided to help finance college costs—particularly for youths from low-income families; whether financial assistance should be given directly to students or their families or to schools in the form of institutional aid; whether support should be provided to students in the form of grants or loans; and the extent to which financial support should be conditioned on income and assets. Relatively little emphasis is typically placed on examining the performance of our education system as a whole or on analyzing the effectiveness of education at all levels as a process for bringing about productive investment in human capital.

The essays in this volume are aimed at a more systematic appraisal of education policy as a whole. That is, the case for policies that were proposed and enacted in 1997 to increase federal financial support for postsecondary education is analyzed in the context of the performance of schooling at other levels, the principal forces that influence college enrollment, and the likely effects on postsecondary schooling of tax credits to help pay out-of-pocket costs.

One of the first questions to consider is whether the most serious problems in education are at the postsecondary level. Evidence and experience suggest that problems are instead concentrated at the elementary and secondary levels. This is where deficiencies in student achievement and public dissatisfaction with the education system show up most strongly. Moreover, our college-level education system seems to perform well by international standards.

In their essays, Eric A. Hanushek and Caroline M. Hoxby both argue that the most serious problems are in schooling below the college level. Hanushek points out that we have always emphasized quantity more than quality for secondary schooling and that recent growth in years of schooling in many other countries poses a challenge to U.S. leadership in educational attainment. In his view, the evidence indicates that simply devoting more resources to elementary and secondary schools is unlikely to be productive but programs designed to improve our understanding of successful approaches might be valuable to point the way toward systemic reforms. Hoxby argues that the greater prevalence of competition at the college level is a major reason why schooling performance below the postsecondary level compares unfavorably with higher education. Although she argues that federal policies can foster productive investment at the postsecondary level, some of it in the form of remedial programs, she warns against policies that might lead higher education to be viewed as an entitlement instead of as an investment.

The increase in the payoff to schooling has resulted in more people getting more schooling. Enrollment in postsecondary schooling right after high school has gone up from less than 50 percent during most of the 1970s to more than 60 percent in recent years. These trends in college enrollment reflect changes in costs such as the decline in earn-

5

ings forgone while attending college, increases in out-of-pocket costs such as tuition and fees, and grants or loans to help pay these costs. Thomas J. Kane reviews evidence on the effects of college tuition levels and need-based grants on enrollment. He also describes and critiques the policies to help pay for postsecondary schooling that were proposed and enacted in 1997. In his view, how to pay college costs for a growing youth cohort will be a significant challenge. Analyses by Kane and by Stephen V. Cameron and James J. Heckman point to only small effects of Pell grants on college enrollment. The evidence suggests larger effects of college tuition levels, however, mainly for enrollment in two-year junior colleges.

The most straightforward interpretation of college enrollment patterns in relation to family income levels is that college enrollment is inhibited by difficulties that youths from low-income families have in financing and paying for out-of-pocket costs. Cameron and Heckman point out that this is only one of several possible interpretations of lower enrollment rates for youths from low-income families, and they assemble evidence that the inability to come up with the money is not the main factor. They examine the entire sequence of enrollment and attainment decisions that youths experience to gain insight into the underlying reasons for differences in enrollment patterns among youths from families with different income levels and different racial and ethnic backgrounds. The evidence that they develop points to long-term family effects, and not cash liquidity constraints, as the main impediments to college enrollment by youths from low-income families. They note that need-based grants are already available to youths from families with the lowest incomes. And since the additional money available to middle-class families under the newly enacted tax credits can be expected to have only small effects on enrollment, about 90 percent of the additional funds represent a transfer to families of youths who would have attended college in the absence of these tax preferences.

College tuition costs have gone up sharply over the years, but it is important to keep these increases in perspective. Only a small proportion of college students go to the elite schools with very high tuition rates, and only a fraction of those who attend these schools pay the full price. Assistance is made available in various forms for low-income students with high qualifications. And although tuition cost increases for public universities have been large in percentage terms, they start from a relatively low base, and tuition cost levels, especially in-state tuition levels, still remain fairly low at most public postsecondary schools. The largest component of total real costs of postsecondary schooling, however, is earnings that are forgone while attending school, and the decline in this component of costs needs to be weighed in relation to increases in other costs. An issue highlighted by Cameron and Heckman in their analysis is the merit of still further subsidization of postsecondary schooling in the context of all the factors influencing payoffs to postsecondary schooling and the increase in enrollment stimulated by higher payoffs and in view of public subsidies that are already large and cover much of the out-of-pocket cost of postsecondary schooling.

References

National Commission on the Cost of Higher Education. 1998. Washington, D.C.: Government Printing Office.

President. 1997. "Address before a Joint Session of the Congress on the State of the Union." *Weekly Compilation of Presidential Documents* 23, no. 6 (February 10): 139.

President's Commission on Higher Education. 1947. *Higher Education for Democracy*. Washington, D.C.: Government Printing Office.

U.S. Bureau of the Census. 1947. Series P-23, no. 173.

U.S. Internal Revenue Service. 1997. Notice 97-60. October 29.

2

Budgets, Priorities, and Investment in Human Capital

Eric A. Hanushek

This volume, which responds to a series of federal education initiatives, provides an opportunity to look at a set of questions that have received surprisingly little attention. These questions involve the issue of where our governmental policy focus in education should be placed. If we begin from a position that we are going to pay attention to education, should we focus on higher education? Should we focus on elementary and secondary schools? Or should we pursue a mixed strategy?

In one sense the general lack of attention is not surprising, because these topics are frequently taken as entirely separate issues, researched by different people and addressed by policy makers of varying fundamental interests. At the same time, it is natural to think that there is some relationship between elementary and secondary schools and higher education. For there is. Unfortunately, we seldom ask the overarching question about how that relationship might influence policy deliberations.

This volume also takes up a second important issue. Contrary to the prevailing Washington perspective, the definition of a given policy is not always synonymous with the resources that are applied to that area. When we are in the middle of intense budget negotiations (as we have continuously been throughout the 1980s and the 1990s), everybody thinks that the most relevant dimension of a policy has to do with the state of agreement between the president and a House or a Senate committee on some numerical figure in a budget document. I submit that this constitutes only a small portion of our education policy, and so should constitute only a small portion of the way we think about education policy.

The context for this discussion is that proposals by the Clinton administration and actions in Congress in 1997 were heavily weighted toward allocating resources for higher education, even though federal financial support was already more important there than for elementary and secondary education. Moreover, virtually the only public debate about higher education policy was about details, such as the mixture between Pell grants and tax deductions. Little consideration went to whether a focus on higher education is appropriate.

To me, the issues are not about the balance of grants and tax preference items for higher education but rather the larger questions, the balance of human capital investment policies. My perspective is a straightforward one. If we compare higher education with elementary and secondary education, higher education appears to be performing quite well and to be the part of our educational system that is working. Our elementary and secondary schools appear not to be working nearly as well. In fact they have substantial problems, even though the policy focus and the federal concern are directed to higher education and not to elementary and secondary education.

The theme of this volume is, How should we think about educational investment strategies? Although it seems implausible on the surface, let's consider what hypothetical circumstances would make disproportionate attention to higher education the correct way to view education policy, given the current state of our educational system.

Background

Educational investments are important for the U.S. economy, and we ought to think about an aggressive human capital investment strategy. The U.S. economy has largely been built upon a skilled labor force and has capitalized on the presence of skills, making human capital investments very important to the success of the general economy. Furthermore, as Kane and Cameron and Heckman show in this volume, the labor market value of the increased skills, as measured by schooling level, has increased dramatically in recent years. This valuation demonstrates that the economy continues to require an increasingly skilled labor force.

Some recent work has suggested, too, that education is crucial to the growth rates of the nation as a whole and that there is an important relationship between human capital and growth rates. Economists have recently spent considerable time and effort trying to understand why some countries grow faster than others, and the majority opinion is that a nation's stock of human capital is an important component of differential growth rates. Moreover, some recent research I have carried out with one of my students suggests to me that the quality of schooling is perhaps the most important component. This finding

9

dovetails with the concerns expressed below about how U.S. quality lags behind that of many countries in the world.

The growth effects are important if we consider the justification for governmental involvement in education, as opposed to purely private decision making on schooling. Governmental intervention is frequently justified on the basis of external benefits—benefits that go beyond the individual investing in the schooling. Are there external benefits to investing in education? Education is often thought to be a "large externality" undertaking, but identification and measurement of those externalities have proved difficult. My proposed candidate for the most important potential external benefit from investing in education is the overarching effect on growth rates that potentially affect the whole economy. The work supporting this hypothesis is not refined; it does not give a precise answer; and numerous qualifications about the external effects of education pervade this volume. Nonetheless, growth effects are certainly an important policy issue to consider.

Next, we have thought of education as a primary ingredient in providing equality of opportunity to society—as a way of cutting down or breaking intergenerational correlations of income and of trying to provide opportunity to all of society. That is the focus, in part, of the discussion on access to higher education, and it is an important reason for us to continue our attention to education.

In terms of total investment, the data show that we have had a consistent focus on education over a long period of time. It is common to hear how important it is that the president focuses attention on education. Implicit or explicit in this observation is the sentiment that we have been shortchanging the educational system. It may be that the president can get the attention of the population better than anybody else, but there has been a consistent policy thrust and a heavy emphasis given to education and human capital investment for a long time. The emphasis has not, however, been given at the federal government level.

The federal government is not the main actor in either elementary and secondary or higher education. For a long time, we have seen considerable growth in the resources from states and localities going into education. President Clinton emphasized provision of more federal support for educational investment by devoting a substantial portion of his 1997 State of the Union address to his proposals. Presidents Reagan and Bush also focused attention on education policy, however. In 1989, for example, President Bush convened a historic gathering of the governors of all the states to focus exclusively on issues of education. They set a series of lofty goals for the year 2000. Unfortunately, we are now very close to the year 2000, and we are not close to meeting

FIGURE 2–1
REAL SPENDING PER STUDENT, 1890–1990

1990 $ per student in thousands

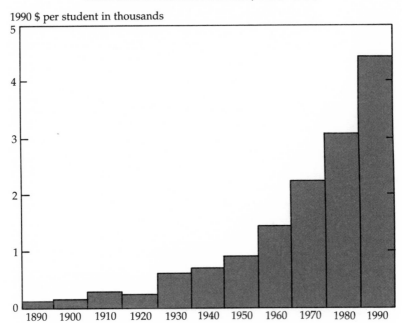

SOURCE: Author.

the goals. Indeed, even if we change "goals 2000" to "goals 2010," I do not believe that we have much chance of achieving them, given current and proposed policies toward schools.

Past Investments in Human Capital. We now turn to the matter of human capital investment, at least as conveyed by spending. I am able to give exact figures regarding elementary and secondary education, for both enrollment and spending. I do not have the comparable numbers for higher education. They are more difficult to get, although Tom Kane has provided some of the basic data.

Figure 2–1 is a display of what has happened to real per pupil spending. Real per pupil spending over a 100-year period has grown at about 3.5 percent per year, that is, after adjusting for inflation. In constant 1990 dollars, spending goes from $170 per student in 1890 to $4,800 per student in 1990. There is simply no getting around the fact that the United States has been investing steadily increasing amounts per pupil in education.

For recent time periods, table 2–1 shows that we have been invest-

11

TABLE 2-1
PUBLIC SCHOOL RESOURCES, 1961–1991

Characteristic	Year						
	1960–61	1965–66	1970–71	1975–76	1980–81	1985–86	1990–91
Pupil-teacher ratio	25.6	24.1	22.3	20.2	18.8	17.7	17.3
Percentage of teachers with master's degrees	23.1	23.2	27.1	37.1	49.3	50.7	52.6
Median years of teacher experience	11	8	8	8	12	15	15
Current expenditure/ ADA (1992–93 $s)	$1,903	$2,402	$3,269	$3,864	$4,116	$4,919	$5,582

SOURCE: Author.

ing in just the way people want to talk about it. For elementary and secondary schools, we have been lowering pupil-to-teacher ratios, we have dramatically increased the average experience of teachers, and we have doubled the percentage of teachers who have master's degrees over the past quarter century. Because we pay for each of these, they add up to a dramatic increase in real spending. From 1960 to 1990, real spending per student almost tripled.

The spending growth has stalled in the 1990s. I interpret this largely as a public reaction to the poor performance from past spending, something that is documented below. It does, however, suggest that public schools are likely to be under increasing fiscal pressures and that they will have to find ways to adjust their behavior in light of this and performance demands.

Higher education data are harder to produce. Nonetheless, this chart of spending can put them in the context of the data that Tom Kane has developed and presents elsewhere in this volume. He has produced data on higher education real spending per full-time equivalent student between 1980 and 1995. These data show that public four-year colleges have a trend in spending growth that is somewhat lower than that for elementary and secondary schools, but that private four-year schools have exhibited a growth trend that is somewhat higher. Because college students predominantly attend public institutions, the average growth in higher education expenditure has been somewhat less than that in elementary and secondary expenditure, but the paths have been quite similar. In other words, the United States has pursued a consistent, across-the-board policy of investing more in education, such that, although significant, recent proposals must be put into the context of a historic commitment to expanding education.

Recent federal budget documents do not reflect a new thrust toward investing in education and human capital. They reflect the fact that the federal government is taking a more serious look at education and concentrating more heavily on higher education. Except for the publicity aspects, however, human capital investment remains chiefly the province of states and localities.

Performance. It is useful to look at performance in the context of the investment of resources. In doing so, it is natural to contrast performance in elementary and secondary education with that in higher education. Beginning with elementary and secondary education, the basic story is simple. In terms of quality of learning, U.S. schools are not now, and have not been, very competitive when judged by the performance of elementary and secondary schools around the world. Fig-

FIGURE 2–2
INTERNATIONAL TEST SCORE PERFORMANCE, FOR
SELECTED COUNTRIES, 1963–1991

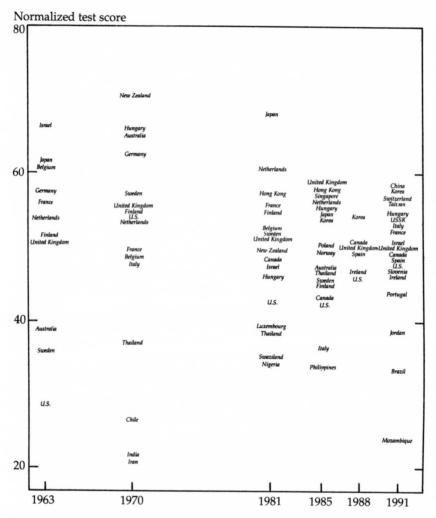

SOURCE: Author.

ure 2–2 presents what we know about all international testing of math
and science scores for U.S. students through the middle of 1996.

This figure depicts years of international testing along the hori-
zontal axis, each column representing a different year. The vertical axis
presents a normalized score, making it possible to compare countries

over time. Each country taking the test in a given year is arrayed according to its score on a scale where the world mean for each testing year is 50.

The U.S. performance varies over time. The drift depicted in the figure closely mirrors the average performance of U.S. seventeen-year-olds on the mathematics and science tests of the National Assessment of Educational Progress (NAEP). Moreover, the key revelation of this figure is that the United States is almost always below the median of whichever group of countries is taking the test.

In 1997, results released for the Third International Math and Science Study (TIMSS) placed U.S. eighth graders right in the middle of the pack. Fourth graders scored higher, but U.S. twelfth graders were at the bottom. This performance, which is not included in the figure, resulted as it did even though a very wide range of countries—forty-one—participated in the testing. Thus, there is no real change in the latest scores.

The fact is that the United States has not been doing particularly well in international comparisons. This may seem surprising, since the United States has an economy built on a skilled labor force. You might ask, "How could that be?" While the United States is not doing well, it is producing skilled goods that one might argue require a skilled labor force. The answer seems to be that over a long period of time we have substituted quantity of schooling for quality. Historically, we have always had a labor force with more years of schooling, on average, even if these years of schooling have been of a lower quality than those of other countries. That quantitative superiority is ending. Table 2–2 compares the percentage of students in different countries that have received upper secondary school education, essentially a high school education. These completion rates are broken down by age. The purpose of breaking them down by age is to be able to read the schooling policies of countries in different years. Individuals who are twenty-five to thirty-four years old in 1992 were educated sometime in the 1980s. People aged thirty-five to forty-four were educated in the 1970s. The next group in the table was educated in the 1960s, and the final group in the 1950s.

Looking at the 1980s, it is clear that a large number of countries are rivaling the 87 percent of U.S. students who are completing high school educations. There are three others in the G-7 group. In the displayed countries outside of the G-7 group, another five are above an 80 percent high school completion rate. That contrasts sharply with earlier decades, when the United States had a dramatic lead in terms of quantity of schooling. There is no getting around the fact that other OECD countries and developing countries have been dramatically in-

15

TABLE 2–2
POPULATION WITH UPPER-SECONDARY-LEVEL EDUCATION,
BY AGE AND COUNTRY, 1992
(in percent)

	Age Group			
	1980s	1970s	1960s	1950s
	25–34	35–44	45–54	55–64
G-7[a]				
Canada	81	78	66	49
France	67	57	47	29
Germany	89	87	81	69
Italy	42	35	21	12
United Kingdom	81	71	62	51
United States	87	88	83	73
Other				
Australia[b]	57	56	51	42
Austria	79	71	65	50
Belgium	60	52	38	24
Czechoslovakia[c]	87	79	68	51
Denmark	67	61	58	45
Finland	82	69	52	31
Ireland	56	44	35	25
Netherlands	68	61	52	42
New Zealand	60	58	55	49
Norway	88	83	75	61
Portugal[c]	21	17	10	7
Spain	41	24	14	8
Sweden	83	76	65	48
Switzerland	87	84	78	70
Turkey	21	14	9	5

a. No data are available for Japan.
b. 1993 data.
c. 1991 data.
SOURCE: Organization for Economic Cooperation and Development, Center for Educational Research and Innovation, International Indicators Project, 1995.

creasing the amount of schooling their youths receive. The U.S. advantage in quantity of schooling is diminishing.

The final part of the story on elementary and secondary education relates to the previous discussion. We have been devoting enormous resources to education but not getting much from these resources. This is the part that leads to the policy conundrum.

Figure 2–3 is a picture of math achievement in the United States as measured by the National Assessment of Educational Process, currently the best yardstick of student performance that we have. The heavy line in the middle reflects the average scores of seventeen-year-olds on the NAEP over time. It shows that now our students are doing about as well as they did in 1970—even though we are spending three-quarters more in real per pupil spending. It shows essentially the same thing for science, except that instead of being flat, the 1994 performance is below the level of 1970. This picture does not lead anyone to believe that our investment policy is soon going to handle the quality concerns and to push us up to the top of the international rankings. "First in the world in math and science in the year 2000" was the statement of the 1989 National Governors' Conference. It does not look like we are on that path.

A second revelation contained in this figure is that there is a substantial gap between whites on the one hand and blacks or Hispanics on the other. That gap has narrowed some, but it remains substantial and recently may even be again widening. This brings us back to the equality of opportunity concerns; it also relates to Heckman and Cameron's discussion in this volume of the importance of the Armed Forces Qualification Test (AFQT) and student achievement in explaining some of the college attendance gaps. Those attendance gaps exist throughout this period and seem to be related to quality of schooling.

The situation with higher education is very different. U.S. higher education is arguably the best in the world. Admittedly, data about higher education are not nearly as good as what we have for elementary and secondary education. It is particularly hard to document quality because we do not have good objective measures. What we do know is:

- U.S. business and industry are willing now to pay a lot more for college graduates than in the past, both in relative terms and in absolute terms.
- Foreign students like to come to U.S. higher educational institutions, whereas none of them want to come to U.S. elementary and secondary schools.
- Employers seem to be a lot better pleased with higher education than they are with elementary and secondary education.

FIGURE 2–3
NAEP Mathematics Achievement Score for Seventeen-Year-Olds, by Race or Ethnicity, 1973–1994

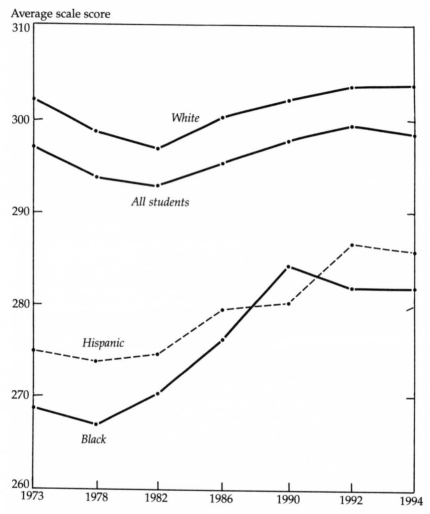

Average scale score

SOURCE: Author.

This adds up to a prima facie case that quality does not appear to be a major problem in higher education—as contrasted with the data displayed earlier, where quality looks like the major concern in elementary and secondary education.

Contemporary Policy Discussion

Having presented this preamble about education issues, I will address the particular policies that have been put forward and discussed at the federal level. I will begin with the proposed elementary and secondary policies and then turn to higher education policies.

My overview of elementary and secondary policies is that they are not very promising. If one looks at the various points made in the president's 1997 foray into elementary and secondary education, one sees a little bit of Internet access, a little bit of ensuring school safety from drugs, a little bit of preschool, and a grab bag of other small items. This was followed by his 1998 emphasis on broad reductions in class size—an apparent effort to duplicate the political popularity of an earlier program to reduce class size in California. It is not a consistent, well-focused policy that one might expect would have a major impact on performance in the schools. The only serious spending component, that for class-size reductions, is not supported by any evidence that would suggest likely performance improvements.

The one feature of the proposals that I do like is the testing and measurement component. I think this is extraordinarily important. We do not know how it might be implemented, but I think it is essential to concentrate systematic attention on these issues. Without better measurement, we will continue to guess about policy without having the type of feedback that is necessary for systemic improvements. Unfortunately, Congress seems little inclined toward expanded testing, in part because of worries about expanded federal intrusions into schools.

The most disappointing aspect of the proposals for me is that nothing is said about the incentives to increase the performance of schools. If we are going to improve our elementary and secondary schools, we have to do something about the incentive structure. Little today directly pushes school personnel to work to increase student achievement or to use resources effectively. There is nothing in this package that has to do with that. The class-size proposals, for example, would maintain the current structure of schools while pursuing a policy that has proved to be an expensive failure.

The other contributors to this volume discuss higher education in detail. In higher education, all the attention is given to the financing of higher education. Nothing is said about quality initiatives, perhaps because few people think that is an issue. I am not going to try to duplicate or repeat the other presentations. They consider the potential impact of the financing elements that have been largely written into law by Congress. The summary statement is simply that you get very little enrollment response from an expensive package of tax subsidies and grants.

That makes the policies a pure transfer program to the current winners of the system. The people who go to college are the current winners, because they can expect to get considerably higher future incomes. In fact, by the usual calculations, the added earnings attributable to obtaining a college degree will much more than pay for the expenses (both tuition and forgone earnings) of attending. Does it not seem strange that the ones who are going to win in the labor market are getting the transfers, so that their advantages are multiplied?

There may be some transfer to schools in a variety of ways. For example, most private schools offer need-based scholarships and need-based aid. Aid is directly tied to the ability-to-pay assessment of the individual student and family. I presume that private schools are changing their estimate of the need of students based on their ability to recoup money from the recent federal government tax and grant policies. Thus, without raising their tuition, private schools will certainly increase their net tuition receipts, simply by pulling back on other forms of aid.

For public schools, tuition bears little relationship to the costs of offering an education. States subsidize attendance through direct budgetary outlays from general tax revenues, and tuition represents the choice of what portion of costs will be borne by the student and what portion by the general taxpayer. All states ultimately trade off subsidies to college students against other possible spending options (such as elementary and secondary schooling or welfare programs). Thus, the development of new federal programs that ease the financial burden on college students and their families will undoubtedly lead some states to consider altering their current subsidies to public colleges and universities. Indeed, in order for public school students in some states to get the full federal subsidy, tuitions must be raised.

Nothing in the package of higher education policies is directed at altering the quality or performance of colleges and universities. It is entirely a fiscal package of financing aimed at individual attendees. There has, however, been some discussion of whether college tuitions have risen "too rapidly," and of whether this set of policies might encourage further tuition increases. With this idea in mind, some of the fiscally minded policy makers in Washington have begun openly questioning the possibility of regulating tuition at colleges and universities.

Putting aside the question of the advisability of the federal government's intrusion (as a minority stockholder in the public colleges of the United States) in tuition setting, this aspect of tuition policy could actually lead to quite undesirable outcomes in terms of the quality and performance of U.S. higher education—the crown jewel of our total education system.

The nature of the federal education policies leads to a simple question: How could such an approach possibly be justified?

The easiest answer to this question might be that nobody really intends the tax credits to be an education policy. Instead, they are simply a device to transfer resources to the middle class, a group always viewed as key in any political coalition. By disguising this as an "education policy," the purely political fiscal action gains respectability and has an arguable social purpose. In other words, it is simply "good politics."

If, however, we do not accept such a simple answer, we are led to think about when it would make sense to concentrate policy attention on higher education. The strategy focuses most of the attention on the part of the system that seems to be working well, and none, or little, of the attention on the part that seems to be working poorly. Is there any way to look at this set of policies as a second-best investment strategy?

There are two reasons why such an approach might appear to make sense—though ultimately I do not believe it does. One rationalization is that we simply lack ideas about how to improve elementary and secondary education, and therefore we should put our resources into the sector that seems to use resources more effectively. I probably contributed to the promotion of this view in that a lot of my work has suggested that there is not a close relationship between the amount of resources pumped into elementary and secondary education and the performance of students. But that is something different. That is why I differentiate between true educational policies and the pure fiscal and financial aspects. I do not think that the correct approach to the problem is to pump more money into education and to call that "human capital development." At the same time, I want to readjust the program to emphasize elementary and secondary more than higher education. What makes these two notions consistent is that I am opposed to creating a huge budget initiative that throws money, blindly, across the system. The purely fiscal solution is something different from good educational policy as sketched below. Class-size reductions, also discussed below, are simply a very directed and inefficient form of resource policies.

A second rationalization of the current policy focus is the view that we must just accept the current restrictions on the educational

21

system. This view begins with the notion that the current woes of the elementary and secondary system are caused by the combination of a heavily unionized work force operating within a heavily regulated sector marked by a series of local monopolies. But instead of focusing attention on that set of more fundamental attributes, the current policy response tries to avoid the sector altogether, on the assumption that reform is just too difficult. In other words, rope off the part of the system that is not working and try to make up for it by expanding the part that is working. Indeed, one cynical perspective on the growing call to make fourteen years of schooling the new standard for all youths is that the two years past high school—if provided by well-functioning schools—could make up for what students had not learned in elementary and secondary schools. (Such an expansion of the quantity of schooling does appear roughly to be obligatory to bring U.S. students near the goal of leading the world in math and science, if we keep the average quality of elementary and secondary schools at the current level.) In the end, our federal education programs are clearly not good educational policy. The higher education parts in the programs do not change people's behavior, being almost exclusively a transfer. They do not affect our large problems of quality at lower levels of education. They simply do not increase the amount of human capital available to the economy. Neither of the two rationalizations offered above seems like a good guide for public policy toward education. Accepting either would likely doom our economy to failed competition against the better-educated, better-prepared labor forces appearing in many other world economies. It is simply too expensive to pursue a policy of expanding upon poor quality. Other countries can easily nullify any such attempts by expanding upon high quality.

Altered Educational Policies

A full discussion of different approaches to developing human capital goes far beyond the scope of this discussion. Again, the key element seems to be changing the incentives in the system, so that students, parents, teachers, and school personnel are more strongly motivated to improve achievement. Some of the options are presented in an earlier report by a group of economists interested in improving elementary and secondary schools—*Making Schools Work: Improving Performance and Controlling Costs,* published by the Brookings Institution in 1994. That report strongly advocated changing the structure of schools to incorporate better incentives.

In the context of this discussion of education policy, however, one cannot easily ignore a central difference between our primary and secondary schools and our colleges and universities. One of the reasons why many people think that U.S. higher education might be doing better than elementary and secondary education is that there is much more competition in higher education than in elementary and secondary education. Part of that competition comes from the way we have chosen to aid students. We give low-income students the resources to go out and shop for a school; that is precisely the mechanism of the Pell grant program. The general prevalence of need-based aid for students with less income also frees choice of schools.

We do not emphasize institutional aid in higher education. Nor do we rely on a paternalistic policy of instructing (regulating) schools to follow the current educational model of how best to educate disadvantaged students who want to pursue higher education. In elementary and secondary education, we do not like those ideas, at least as one can infer by policies. Although the president has indicated some favor for competition in schools, little consistent policy development has followed. Nor has draft legislation been developed. Any policy support falls far short of a Pell grant for disadvantaged students in elementary and secondary schools. Making the distinction between vouchers for higher education and vouchers for lower levels of education on conceptual grounds takes considerable effort and is usually not successful. This fact might reflect the restrictions on the way elementary and secondary schools are organized and run, or it might fit into the noneducational interpretation of the currently proposed policies—it is good politics, as opposed to good educational policy.

An Appropriate Federal Role

An important element to this discussion, nonetheless, is consideration of what the federal government's role should be. Even though education is primarily the responsibility of states and localities, the federal government has some strong and obvious roles.

Perhaps at the top of the list is providing leadership in policy development and evaluation. Since all states can benefit from increased knowledge about how to improve schools, there is a natural advantage to the centralization of expertise and research direction (offset, of course, by the possibility of myopic or inefficient "monopolist" programs). The past history on this score has not been encouraging, however, as the federal government's research program has had limited success in expanding our knowledge.

A closely related potential model for the federal government would be the development of a directed program of knowledge acquisition, patterned after, say, the National Institutes of Health. NIH has developed a program of serious scientific inquiry into how the health of the population can be improved. Among the components of this program are the extensive use of random-assignment experiments in areas where the full description of how treatments interact with health have eluded us. Adaptation of this approach to education has considerable merit.

We had, in the past, a program of social experimentation in labor supply, in health insurance, in housing, and in a variety of other areas. These social experimentation programs of the 1960s and 1970s provided us with a lot of information about the effects of various public policies and the best ways to conduct random-assignment experimentation. We have not run major experiments since then.

The case for more random-assignment experimentation has been made frequently. Under a range of circumstances, such experimentation promises clearer answers in situations where complicated individual processes are not fully understood and thus cannot be modeled well in statistical analyses. This approach seems particularly appropriate for investigating the effects of alternative incentive structures in schools.

The kinds of policies that will be most effective in schools are the ones that involve changing incentives, so that participants in the system have a stake in the performance of students. One way or another, we need resources to flow toward good performance and away from bad performance, something that does not happen now. In fact, the opposite may often be the case currently.

Unfortunately, we do not know much about how to introduce performance incentives, as they have not been used extensively or evaluated. Thus, we are not building on much information.

Incentive design is easy to motivate in terms of vouchers. There have been broad discussions about whether vouchers are good or bad, but these discussions so far have been abstract and far removed from a discussion of the details of any policy. The discussion of vouchers often looks like a debate contrasting the conceptual ideals of a Communist system against the reality of a mixed capitalist system. On conceptual grounds, the Communist system can always be described as dealing with the undesirable aspects of the capitalist system, even though there is little doubt about the superiority of the capitalist system as compared with whatever Communist system is actually implemented. Similarly, vouchers have considerable conceptual appeal. But we do not know how to structure them in actual schooling situations. One could, for example, think of voucher structures that lead to the significant stratification of society on racial or economic grounds, that promote schools with little academic content, or that lead to other undesirable outcomes. We have to consider alternative detailed structures of vouchers and evaluate them. This is precisely the kind of issue for which experimental methods could prove useful.

Vouchers represent just one possible incentive structure. We have, for example, performance-contracting structures that invite private provision of educational services. We have the current rush to charter schools that alter the governance and incentive structure. And we have traditional favorites, like merit pay for teachers. We currently do not know how to organize these alternatives to get the promised benefits without undesirable outcomes. This is an obvious arena in which the federal government can show leadership. The simplest way to provide leadership within the current system of state responsibility would be through serious experimentation with alternative incentive structures and serious evaluation of the results.

The federal government further has an obvious role in expanding opportunities and equity in the system. NAEP scores in the past have demonstrated, for example, significant differences in performance between samples of students who are white, African American, and Hispanic. If we also consider the Cameron and Heckman analysis, which shows the importance of student achievement in terms of college attendance, the larger problem is immediately evident. Disparities in achievement will translate into significant disparities in economic outcomes. The federal government should address some of these concerns.

Indeed, historically the federal government has emphasized the education of disadvantaged students in terms of its budgetary outlays. Large portions of the federal spending on education have been means-tested and aimed at lower-income groups. The recently enacted higher education programs, while income-conditioned, generally increase spending much higher on the income scale than formerly. The breadth of spending makes it difficult to say that it is really directed at needy students.

It is interesting again to contrast the federal perspective in higher education with that in elementary and secondary education. The primary approach to providing aid to disadvantaged students in higher education is the Pell grant, an income-contingent voucher that can be taken to the student's school of choice—whether public or private, religious or sectarian. The primary approach to providing aid to disadvantaged students in elementary and secondary schools is Title I funding—institutional aid to school systems based on the number of disadvantaged students they have. In the thirty years of compensatory education funding at the elementary and secondary level, there has been little indication of any generally favorable outcomes in terms of student performance. With higher education, while there are concerns about the use of Pell grants at some proprietary schools, little general concern is expressed about the possibility that disadvantaged students are not being significantly aided. Perhaps again we should consider how elementary and secondary education and higher education might be related in policy.

The federal government can and, frankly, should be actively involved in developing a clear human capital policy. Nonetheless, a more focused role than is currently pursued would be more in keeping with prevailing views about the division of responsibility between public and private sector entities and between different levels of government.

Conclusions

Education is important to the U.S. economy, and the federal government should participate in developing policies to encourage human capital development. The federal government should also be concerned about providing equal opportunities to students. These ideas are straightforward and subject to little controversy.

But the mere fact of having a large budget item related to some education program is not sufficient. Recent federal actions have introduced significant tax subsidies and expenditures related to students attending colleges and universities. The best information currently available, however, suggests that few new students will be attracted to college as a result of the subsidy package—implying that this should be viewed mainly as a transfer to students who would otherwise attend college, not as a program designed to change the human capital development of our youths.

That focus has an even more questionable aspect. Today's concern about education is centered on the quality of elementary and secondary schools, while colleges and universities are generally viewed as being quite successful. The logic required to direct policy chiefly at the successful part of the system while ignoring the less successful part is very strained. Perhaps the best argument would involve an admission of defeat in terms of reforming elementary and secondary schools. This argument would then suggest hiring colleges to provide remedial instruction to make up for what the earlier schools did not provide. I believe it is premature to give up on reforming elementary and secondary schools, even though I am also convinced that purely budgetary approaches will not work. Nor will continuation and expansion of past policies that have not proved successful—such as broad reductions in class size.

My own preference, based on an examination of past efforts to help schools, would be for the federal government to become much more active in developing the knowledge base for effective reform. In the simplest terms, turning even a small portion of tax breaks and subsidies for higher education into a systematic experimentation effort holds much more promise for improving the human capital of our youths than recent policies.

Programs of experimentation and evaluation do not, however, have the same political appeal as transferring federal funds to middle-class families. And advertising tax breaks as supporting the education of our youths has the advantage of wrapping a political fiscal policy in an American flag. That appears to be the trade-off: short-run political gain for long-run development of the national economy.

3
Where Should Federal Education Initiatives Be Directed?

Caroline M. Hoxby

How should we strike the balance of priorities between higher education and primary and secondary education in federal policy? This question is not asked frequently, but it is one of the utmost importance in making budgetary decisions. In each of the Clinton administration's budgets for 1998 through 2000, the vast majority of the initiatives related to education dealt with primary and secondary education. Each budget contained scarcely any new initiatives for higher education. Yet, a count of the initiatives can be misleading. Appropriations and tax expenditures for higher education represented 75 percent of the new education spending in 1998. The emphasis was reversed in 1999, when 40 percent of the new education spending went to higher education. The budget for 2000 is rather balanced: proposed appropriations and tax expenditures for higher education represent 45 percent of new education. See tables 3–1, 3–2, and 3–3 for summaries of education-related spending in, respectively, fiscal year 1998 and fiscal year 1999 and the budget for fiscal year 2000. In which year—1998, 1999, or 2000—has the federal government achieved the right balance between initiatives for higher education and initiatives for primary and secondary education?

Any response requires an answer to a related question: Is the higher education sector as troubled as elementary and secondary education, and if not, what makes the two sectors function differently? This chapter will attempt to address that fundamental question and then to explain the implications the answer has for some specific federal education initiatives.

Differences between Primary-Secondary and Higher Education

Why is it that American higher education functions differently from primary and secondary education in the United States? In particular,

28

TABLE 3–1
EDUCATION-RELATED APPROPRIATIONS AND TAX EXPENDITURES,
FISCAL YEAR 1998
(in billions of dollars)

School construction	1.000
Special education	0.774
Technology literacy challenge funds and technology innovation challenge grants	0.264
Disadvantaged students (Title I)	0.181
Bilingual education	0.092
Innovative education program strategies	0.040
Charter schools	0.030
Teacher professional development	0.025
Total K–12 appropriations and tax expenditures	2.406
Hope and lifelong learning tax credits	5.600
Pell grants	0.932
Education IRAs	0.300
Miscellaneous tax expenditures for higher education	0.200
Tax deduction of student loan interest	0.100
Other postsecondary financial aid	0.023
Total postsecondary appropriations and tax expenditures	7.155

SOURCE: Author.

why is it that the higher education sector appears to be so much more productive and successful than the elementary and secondary school sector? (See chapter 2 in this volume.) The answer lies in the fact that these two sectors have different market structures. Higher education in the United States is competitive, in three significant ways. College students have much more decision-making power about where they will attend college because they are more flexible geographically than elementary and secondary students. Also, private institutions offer many more viable and more numerous options at the college level than at the primary and secondary levels. Finally, and perhaps most significantly, college students and their families shoulder more of the burden of paying for their own educations than do their counterparts in the primary and secondary sector. This additional responsibility encourages better performance on the part of the students, and more competition among colleges for the students' prized dollars. Each of these factors can be analyzed in its own right.

The Competitiveness of the Market for College Education. Increasingly, students choose from an array of institutions of higher education

TABLE 3–2
EDUCATION-RELATED APPROPRIATIONS AND TAX EXPENDITURES,
FISCAL YEAR 1999
(in billions of dollars)

Class-size reduction	1.200
Innovative education program strategies	0.375
Disadvantaged students (Title I)	0.301
Reading improvement	0.260
Teacher professional development and recruitment	0.185
Afterschool programs	0.160
Increasing awareness of and preparation for undergraduate programs	0.120
Reducing violence and drug activity in schools	0.060
Charter schools	0.020
Technology centers and technology innovation challenge grants	0.019
Total K–12 appropriations and tax expenditures	2.700
Hope and lifelong learning tax credits (no policy change, estimated change in tax expenditures)	1.000
Pell grants	0.360
Education IRAs (no policy change, estimated change in tax expenditures)	0.200
Other postsecondary financial aid	0.150
Tax deduction of student loan interest (no policy change, estimated change in tax expenditures)	0.100
Institutional development	0.034
Total postsecondary appropriations and tax expenditures	1.844

SOURCE: Author.

when they decide where to spend their tuition money. While some students are so geographically bound by personal circumstances that they can choose only among colleges in their metropolitan area, many other students consider colleges anywhere within their region or within the United States. Table 3–4 shows three indicators of how the American market for college education has grown more geographically competitive since 1950. In 1950, the average college in the United States faced direct competition from only about thirty other colleges. Today's average college draws students from fourteen states and faces direct competition from about eighty-five other colleges. On the basis of any conventional measure of market competitiveness, colleges in the 1990s function in a competitive environment.

The average primary and secondary school in the United States

TABLE 3–3
EDUCATION-RELATED APPROPRIATIONS AND TAX EXPENDITURES,
BUDGET FOR FISCAL YEAR 2000
(in billions of dollars)

Afterschool programs	0.400
Disadvantaged students (Title I)	0.320
Reading improvement	0.260
Class-size reduction	0.200
Special education	0.166
School construction	0.146
Increasing awareness of and preparation for undergraduate programs	0.135
Teacher professional development and recruitment	0.122
Technology literacy challenge funds and technology centers	0.080
Comprehensive school reform demonstrations	0.030
Charter schools	0.030
Reducing violence and drug activity in schools	0.027
Total K–12 appropriations and tax expenditures	1.916
Student financial aid (not otherwise listed below)	1.875
Work-study	0.064
Institutional development	0.036
College completion challenge grants	0.035
D.C. resident tuition support	0.017
Hope and lifelong learning tax credits (no policy change, estimated change in tax expenditures)	−0.200
Pell grants (increase in maximum grant combined with use of previous years' surpluses)	−0.241
Total postsecondary appropriations and tax expenditures	1.586

SOURCE: Author.

does not face nearly as much competition, for several reasons. The median metropolitan area in the United States has only four school districts—that is, parents can choose among only four possible elementary and secondary school districts. Of course, there is much variation among metropolitan areas in the number of school districts available. A few metropolitan areas have hundreds. About 18 percent of metropolitan areas have only one school district. Clearly, the typical school district does not face as much competition as the typical college faces to attract students and parents.

In addition, parents are relatively constrained in their choices among school districts. Even if many districts exist, switching between them usually requires a change of residence—which can be costly.

TABLE 3–4
INCREASING COMPETITIVENESS OF THE U.S. MARKET FOR
BACCALAUREATE EDUCATION, 1949–1994
(percent)

	1949	1963	1968	1981	1994
Students who attended college in state					
All colleges	93.2	85.1	82.9	77.3	74.5
Private colleges	80.0	68.2	65.6	62.0	54.6
Public colleges	95.6	90.8	90.1	89.7	84.0
Baccalaureate-granting colleges that drew students from					
40 or more states	2.4	6.2	6.5	6.8	7.3
20 or more states	16.2	25.2	26.1	26.7	35.5
Herfindahl indexes for colleges, showing concentration of their students' states of residence					
All colleges	0.79	0.71	0.67	0.64	0.59
Private colleges	0.62	0.53	0.49	0.47	0.41
Public colleges	0.96	0.91	0.87	0.84	0.77

NOTE: This table shows statistics for baccalaureate-granting colleges only. Two-year colleges are not included. The statistics are based on the author's calculations from the panel of baccalaureate-granting colleges in the Residence and Migration surveys of the U.S. Department of Education (U.S. Office of Education, U.S. Bureau of Education). See Hoxby (1997a) for details.
SOURCE: Author.

Choosing an elementary and secondary school district is simply a more constrained choice than choosing a college.

Finally, the amount of competition in primary and secondary education has decreased significantly over time in the United States. The first reason is school district consolidation. In 1950, there were more than 85,000 school districts in the United States. The nation now has fewer than 15,000 school districts. That amounts to almost a sixfold decrease in the number of school districts in the United States. Of course, many of the districts that were consolidated were rural, and their consolidation may not have had much effect on the competitiveness of elementary and secondary education. But the number of metropolitan school districts fell by more than 200 percent since 1950, and their consolidation has undoubtedly affected parents' degree of choice. Figure 3–1 shows the contrast between the rising market competitiveness of higher education and the falling market competitiveness of K–12 education over the post–World War II period.

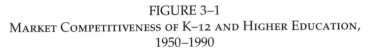

FIGURE 3–1
MARKET COMPETITIVENESS OF K–12 AND HIGHER EDUCATION,
1950–1990

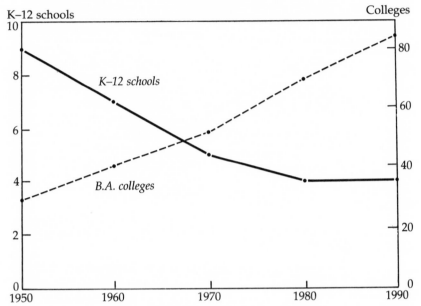

NOTE: Vertical axes represent average numbers of schools or colleges competing.
SOURCE: Author.

The second reason that competition has decreased over time in the elementary and secondary sector is the gradual elimination of local school finance. In 1940, the typical school district in the United States raised just under 70 percent of the money it spent. Most of the money was raised through local property taxes, and districts therefore had to be responsible to local homeowners and voters. A district that used its money inefficiently was likely to experience falling housing prices, low voter support for bond issues, falling property tax revenues, and tight school budgets. In contrast, the typical 1990s school district in the United States relies primarily on the state for its funding. Currently, 57 percent of the average school's funding comes from state and federal governments. As a result, school districts do not compete so hard for local public support. If a school district wants to obtain a generous budget, it may do better by focusing its attention on pleasing the state legislature rather than pleasing local parents. Figure 3–2 shows how

33

FIGURE 3–2

SHARE OF REVENUES TO K–12 SCHOOLS FROM LOCAL SOURCES, 1950–1990

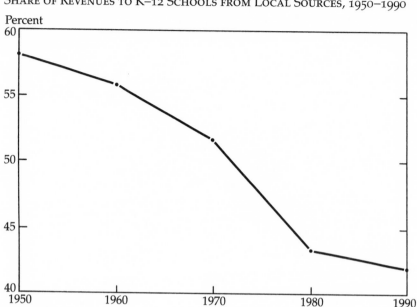

Percent

SOURCE: Author.

the share of revenues from local sources has declined in K–12 education since 1950.

As an aside, note that state and local governments together fund approximately 94 percent of K–12 education. The federal government funds only the remaining 6 percent. Of that 6 percent, the vast majority is spent on Title I, special and bilingual education, and other programs that serve designated student populations. The federal government has only limited control from year to year over how much money these programs absorb. Only about 1 percent of K–12 spending is typically accounted for by federal money that is *really* discretionary. In and of itself, this might make us wonder whether federal programs in K–12 education are likely to have much sway over what schools actually do. Certainly, the economic theory of fiscal federalism suggests that there will be little real effect when a higher level of government gives subsidies to a lower level that account for so little of the lower level's budget. For this reason alone, the federal government may be better off focusing its initiatives on higher education, where its subsidies are much more important. Figure 3–3 shows the federal share of both K–12 expenditures and higher expenditures from 1965 to the present.

FIGURE 3–3
FEDERAL SHARE OF K–12 AND HIGHER EDUCATION REVENUES,
1960–1990

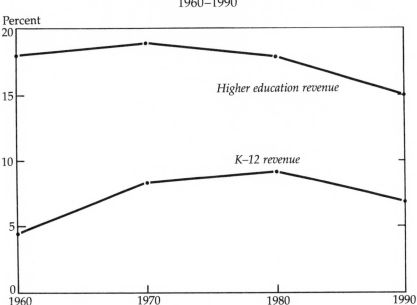

SOURCE: Author.

The third and final reason that competition has decreased in elementary and secondary schooling is teachers' unionization. Teachers unionized in the United States after 1965 and mostly before 1985. Because they have monopoly power in the market for teachers, they make it difficult for public schools to compete fiercely. Figure 3–4 shows two measures of teachers' unionization in the United States from 1960 to the current day.

Private versus Public Financing. The second major difference between the higher education sector and the elementary and secondary sector is that private schools provide significant competition in higher education but much less competition in elementary and secondary education. Private colleges and universities have enrolled approximately 45 percent of college students in most years since World War II. Most college-bound students in the United States have their choice of several private as well as public colleges. Thus, nearly every public college faces some private competitors for its students.

Figure 3–5 shows that the private sector has only a small share

35

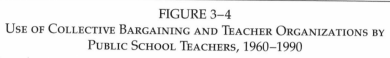

FIGURE 3–4
USE OF COLLECTIVE BARGAINING AND TEACHER ORGANIZATIONS BY
PUBLIC SCHOOL TEACHERS, 1960–1990

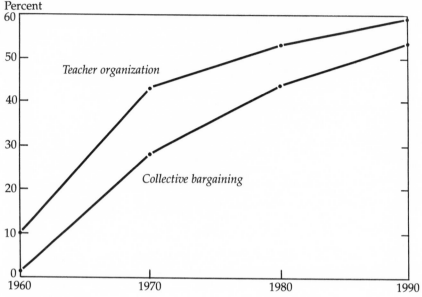

SOURCE: Author.

of elementary and secondary education relative to its share of higher education. Since 1970, private schools have enrolled about 10 percent of American elementary and secondary school students. In 1960, however, this percentage was just above 12 percent. The percentage declined primarily because Catholics increasingly moved away from central cities and became dispersed in the suburbs, where they were less likely to support Catholic schools. Since Catholic schools were the most accessible private schools for working and middle-class parents, the availability of private alternatives in elementary and secondary schooling fell particularly rapidly for middle-income families. That is, private schooling has not just declined as a percentage of total students; the private schooling that remains is oriented toward the most well-off and the least well-off students. The availability of private alternatives is, therefore, another reason why the market structure of higher education and K–12 education has increasingly diverged over time.

Student Investment. The final difference between higher education and elementary and secondary education, one that must be factored

FIGURE 3–5
ENROLLMENT AT PRIVATE K–12 AND HIGHER EDUCATION SCHOOLS,
1960–1990

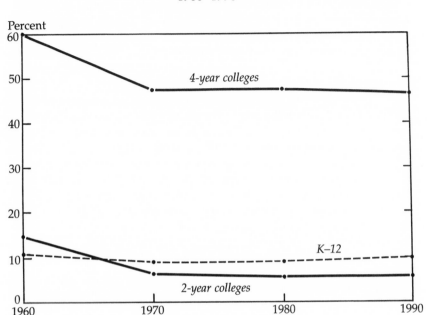

SOURCE: Author.

into any policy decision, is that college students have a much greater degree of financial interest in their attendance decisions than elementary and secondary students have in theirs.

In higher education, students choose not only the school they are going to attend; they usually choose to spend some of their own money. Spending their own money and being responsible for their own choices appear to force students to "wake up" about the importance of education. Students who did not care very much about whether the educational investments they were making in secondary school were productive suddenly start to care when some of the money invested is their own money. Whether it is work opportunities, consumption, or savings that are sacrificed, students do generally make financial sacrifices to attend college, even inexpensive community colleges. Because they have alternative uses for the funds, students quickly become alert to the question of whether they are earning a sufficient return to college. Having to make this calculation routinely appears to affect the seriousness with which they regard education.

37

In public primary and secondary schools, students do not similarly see that they need to earn a return on the money that is being invested in their education. For example, a student in the median central city district in the United States is receiving an education that costs approximately $6,200 (1995–1996). If he is at all typical, that student does not worry much about whether the money is well spent. Yet $6,200 is a much larger sum than the maximum Pell grant has ever contained; and, just a few years after secondary school, the same student would be very grateful for such a large Pell grant or an additional year of Pell grant eligibility. In students' minds, elementary and secondary school expenditure is not parallel to Pell grant expenditure— *even though both are pure subsidies to the individual student.* This is because the Pell grant is fungible (it can be spent at nearly any college) and it is an amount that can be spent only once (a student runs through his Pell grant eligibility). In contrast, secondary school expenditure is not fungible (it belongs to the school rather than to the student, for all practical purposes), and it is available so long as the student makes the minimal effort required to stay in school.

Market Structure, Especially Competition, Determines Performance

The reason I am concerned about the three differences in market structure that I have highlighted is that, in my research, I have found evidence to suggest that market structure determines how well both schools and students perform.

For instance, in addition to having found that the market for college education has experienced steadily increasing competition since 1940 (Hoxby 1997a), I have found empirically that the increase in competition has caused colleges to raise quality, to differentiate themselves by tailoring their programs, and generally to work harder at attracting students (Hoxby 1997b). The well-known colleges that compete for the most able students in the national market have raised their quality of instruction, improved noninstructional aspects of student life, and increasingly subsidized education with endowment money. Many other baccalaureate colleges have reacted to competition by finding their own comparative advantage and creating a market niche—for instance, catering to managers who want to obtain their MBAs without taking time off from working. Colleges of modest selectivity have led the way in developing up-to-date career counseling, cooperative programs with local employers, schedules that suit working students, and services for students with unusual needs (such as immigrants).

Competition among colleges is far more intense than competition among K–12 schools. I have also found, however, that public K–12 schools perform better where they face more competition. For instance, a substantial increase in the degree of competition among public school districts in a metropolitan area makes public K–12 schools more productive: student test scores rise by 3 percent even while costs fall by 17 percent (Hoxby 1997a).[1] In other empirical work (Hoxby 1997b), I have shown that public schools offer higher quality education for cost when they are located in metropolitan areas where they face more competition from private schools. This means that *public* school students benefit from living in an area with competition from private schools. If a public school student lives in a metropolitan area where private schools have a 10 percent larger "market share,"[2] public school students have achievement scores that are eight percentage points higher, attain almost two additional years of higher education, and earn wages that are 12 percent higher.

In other empirical research, I have shown that parents are more active and involved in their children's schooling when they live in metropolitan areas where they have choice among public school districts (Hoxby 1996). This evidence confirms the theory that the action of choosing among schools gives families a sense of ownership and responsibility for the quality of the education they receive. Of course, this theory carries over to higher education, where much more choice is exercised. Alumni donations certainly suggest that college graduates feel a sense of ownership of and responsibility for the colleges they chose. Table 3–5 summarizes some of my findings on the effects of competition on elementary and secondary schooling.

Finally, and perhaps most profoundly, market structure affects how people think about education. Empirically, we know that people think about K–12 education as an entitlement, but think about higher education as an investment choice that individuals make. These different patterns of thought are important because there is evidence that students are less engaged in their schooling when they regard it as

---

1. By "substantial," I mean an increase of two standard deviations in the degree of competition among public school districts, where the degree of competition is measured either by the number of districts per student or the Herfindahl index of enrollment concentration. To give a sense of the magnitude, this "substantial" change corresponds to a metropolitan area going from four to twenty school districts.

2. Private schools' "market share" is their percentage of K–12 enrollment. To obtain empirical evidence on this topic, it is essential to identify the portion of private schools' market share that is driven by exogenous forces rather than the success or failure of local public schools. See Hoxby (1994b) for an econometric strategy for obtaining this type of evidence.

TABLE 3–5
EFFECTS OF COMPETITION ON ELEMENTARY
AND SECONDARY SCHOOLING

Effects	Change
Effects of competition among public school districts[a]	
Effect on per pupil spending	decrease, 17%
Effect on student achievement as measured by test scores	improvement, 3rd percentile point
Effect on student achievement as measured by wages	increase, 4%
Effect on student achievement as measured by educational attainment	0.4 additional years of education
Effect on parents' involvement in their student's school career	increase in parents' visits to schools, 30%
Effects of competition for public schools from private schools[b]	
Effect on public schools' per pupil spending	approximately 0
Effect on achievement of public school students as measured by test scores	improvement, 8th percentile point
Effect on achievement of public school students as measured by wages	increase, 12%
Effect on achievement of public school students as measured by educational attainment	increase in probability of college graduation, 12%

NOTE: Smaller effects are found for metropolitan areas in which school districts do not have financial autonomy (most revenue is state determined).
a. These effects consider an increase of one standard deviation in the number of school districts in a metropolitan area or a decrease of one standard deviation in the concentration of enrollment among school districts in a metropolitan area.
b. These effects consider an increase in exogenous tuition subsidies of $1,000 or an increase in exogenous private school enrollment of 10%.
SOURCE: Author.

an entitlement. For instance, when mandatory schooling laws made graduating from high school the norm, secondary schooling lost its status as a strong indicator of a student's ability and willingness to learn (Owen 1995). High school graduation is now so regarded as an entitlement (by all except students from highly disadvantaged backgrounds) that a middle-class student who wants to signal his job-readiness or ability must complete at least some college. (See Costrell [1995] and Somanathan [1995] for economic models that support this statement.) In other words, there is always a risk inherent in attempting to make a particular level of education universal. Pressuring schools to provide a certain level of education to everyone tends to make that level an entitlement and raises the amount of education that a student must acquire in order to signal his skills.

Differences in Productivity between the K–12 and College Sectors

Significant implications follow from the fact that institutions of higher education systemically experience a different market structure from that of K–12 schools. Perhaps the most important implication is that American higher education is much more productive than is K–12 education—that is, it creates more learning for each dollar expended. It is difficult to measure schools' productivity, but two telling pieces of evidence suggest that colleges are more productive than are K–12 schools. The first is that U.S. higher education is very attractive to foreigners, even foreigners from other G-7 countries.[3] The United States is a net exporter of higher education services, and the exporting is done not just by elite research universities but also by public and private liberal arts colleges and by community colleges. Currently, the number of foreign nationals on student visas is 11 percent in graduate study, 5 percent in private four-year colleges, 4 percent in public four-year colleges, and 3 percent in public two-year colleges. These percentages do not include any foreign-born students who are permanent U.S. residents—if they did, the percentage of foreign-born students in two-year colleges, for instance, would quadruple.[4] Figure 3–6 shows how U.S. *net* exports of college education have grown over the recent period. The fact that American institutions of higher education are net exporters indicates that they provide good value for money by world standards.

In contrast, as Hanushek shows in his chapter in this volume,

---

3. The G-7 are Canada, France, Germany, Italy, Japan, the United States, and the United Kingdom.

4. These figures are the author's calculations, based on the National Postsecondary Student Aid Survey, 1992.

FIGURE 3–6
GROWTH OF U.S. NET EXPORTS OF HIGHER EDUCATION, 1970–1995

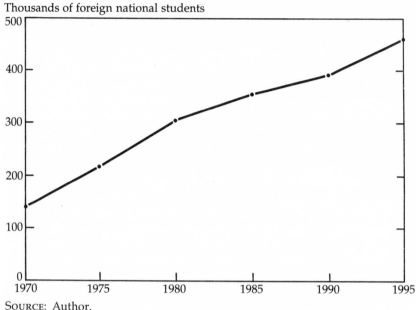

Thousands of foreign national students

SOURCE: Author.

American K–12 schools are poor competitors internationally. They have the highest per-pupil costs among the highly industrialized nations, yet the performance of American K–12 students in this group of countries is middling.

Another indication that the American higher education sector is more productive than the K–12 sector comes from their different cost growth. Between 1970 and 1990, per-pupil costs in K–12 education grew by 71 percent in real (inflation-adjusted) terms. Over the same period, the real cost growth in higher education was 34 percent—less than half the rate of growth in K–12 schooling. Similarly, between 1970 and 1990, college faculty salaries grew about half as fast as K–12 public school teacher salaries. (Note that the popular press creates a distorted picture of higher education costs by focusing on the "list price" tuitions of elite colleges and universities.)

Implications for the Federal Initiatives on Education

Given all the evidence discussed above, should federal education policy focus on higher education, as it has done traditionally and did in fiscal year 1998? Or should the federal government shift its focus toward primary and secondary schooling, as in fiscal year 1999? For two reasons, the traditional focus on higher education is a better use of federal money. First, as described above, the federal government would have to commit *much* more money than it currently contemplates if it wanted to have a significant influence on primary and secondary education. Second, despite being less troubled than the primary and secondary education sector, the higher education sector is a better target for federal programs because its market structure increases the opportunity for *productive* interventions. One way of noting the differences in market structure between the two sectors is noting the differences in the federal initiatives themselves. Federal initiatives for primary and secondary education give funds to schools. But, as we will see, most federal initiatives for higher education give funds to students, who must still participate in the college market. They must choose among types of college programs, select colleges worthy of receiving their funds, and be accepted by colleges into the programs they seek to attend.

One way to use higher education to improve American education *generally* is to allow it to provide a larger share of schooling. Colleges have proven to be efficient education providers for people whose secondary schools were inadequate. Breneman (1997) shows that American colleges, particularly two-year colleges, provide a good deal of remedial schooling at less than half the expense of the secondary schools for which they are substituting. Data from the National Postsecondary Student Aid Survey suggest that among college students who come from below-median-income families, about 35 percent do remedial secondary school work while in college.[5] This amount of remediation suggests not only that American secondary schools are failing a large number of students, but that the best way to help these students may be expanding their access to colleges.

But the higher education sector need not be used merely as a remediator. Lowering financial barriers to higher education can also be a lever for quality improvements in elementary and secondary schools. Minnesota's program provides a good example of how expanding college access can provide K–12 schools with financial incentives to improve. In Minnesota, secondary school students can attend college courses using money that would otherwise be spent by their secondary schools. This has multiple beneficial effects. By making secondary school funds somewhat fungible, the program encourages students to

---

5. These are the author's calculations, using the National Postsecondary Student Aid Survey (1992).

recognize the investment being made in their human capital. By giving students a schooling alternative they might not otherwise have, students can make more productive use of the money allocated to their education. Most important, the program puts some competitive pressure on secondary schools to offer quality education. The current scale of the program is such that these incentive effects are modest, at best, but the potential of such programs is clear.

Historically, colleges have also sometimes acted as curriculum setters and quality evaluators for American secondary schools. States' flagship universities, for instance, were often founded partly with the intention of providing secondary school students and secondary schools with achievement and curricular goals. For instance, Goldin (forthcoming) documents the role of state universities' preparatory schools in setting curricular examples for state secondary schools. This is still a role that colleges *could* play, and the federal government could provide assistance by offering programs that especially decrease students' financial barriers to attending colleges that set high academic standards for admission.

Policy makers must be cautious, however, that their programs for higher education do not actually interfere with those aspects of the higher education sector that make it more successful in the first place. For instance, they should be very cautious about policies that turn higher education into an entitlement instead of an investment. Interventions, which in practice mainly take the form of subsidies, should attempt to move students toward making *more optimal* investments (by relieving liquidity constraints and capital market imperfections), not toward *ignoring* the investment consequences of education. Policy makers should also be cautious about policies that interfere with competition among colleges or the financial consequences of that competition. These points can be used to evaluate higher education policies.

The Higher Education Initiatives in the 1998 Federal Budget

By far the most important new initiatives for higher education in recent years began in 1998. In new education-related spending in that year, the largest items were the tax credits called the Hope credit and the tax credit for lifelong learning. Combined, these are expected to cost $31 billion in fiscal years 1998 through 2002. The Hope credit subsidizes an individual's first two years of undergraduate education by giving him a tax credit worth 100 percent of the first $1,000 plus 50 percent of the second $1,000 he spends on tuition and fees for the first two years of college. Thus, the maximum Hope credit is $1,500 per year. The Hope credit is a modified descendant of the Hope scholarship that President Clinton first proposed in his 1997 State of the Union address.

The tax credit for lifelong learning can be used for any year of undergraduate or graduate education. It provides 20 percent of tuition and fees up to $5,000 through 2002, and 20 percent of tuition and fees up to $10,000 thereafter. The maximum tax credit is, thus, $1,000 through 2002, and $2,000 after 2002. Both the Hope credit and the tax credit for lifelong learning are nonrefundable and phase out for individuals earning $40,000 to $60,000 a year, or couples earning $80,000 to $100,000 a year. The tax credit for lifelong learning is the descendant of President Clinton's proposal for a middle-class tax deduction for college tuition of up to $10,000 a year.

Penalty-free withdrawals from individual retirement accounts (IRAs) to pay for college expenses are a policy that has been proposed perennially since the Bush administration. They were finally enacted to commence in 1998, as part of the Taxpayer Relief Act of 1997. Distributions from an IRA that pay for college expenses are not penalized. In addition, commencing in 1998, new, tax-sheltered college savings accounts or education IRAs (EIRAs) are allowed. EIRAs are like the new (Roth) IRAs in the tax treatment they give to withdrawals for college expenses. The *only* expense for which they can be used without attracting a penalty, however, is college expense. A family may contribute up to $500 a year to an EIRA for each dependent child under the age of nineteen. Penalty-free withdrawals from IRAs for college expenses and EIRAs phase out for families earning $150,000 to $160,000 a year.

The other major tax expenditure for higher education commencing in 1998 is the tax deduction for interest paid on student loans. This is an above-the-line deduction, so whether or not they itemize, borrowers may deduct their interest up to $1,000 in 1998. The maximum deduction rises in $500 increments to $2,500 in 2001. The tax deduction phases out for families earning $60,000 to $75,000 a year.

Finally, the maximum Pell grant was raised from $2,700 a year to $3,000 a year in 1998. It was then raised to $3,125 in 1999, and the budget for 2000 proposes raising it to $3,250. The Pell grant pays tuition, fees, and some living expenses for poor students enrolled in college. The grant that each student receives is a function of his family's income, assets, and composition; the tuition, fees, and other expenses of his college; and the maximum Pell grant.

As for coordination among the higher education initiatives, only *one* of the following four tax claims can be made for a student in a given year: distribution from an IRA or an EIRA, deduction of interest paid on student loans, the tax credit for lifelong learning, or the Hope credit. Any of the four claims can be combined with the Pell grant, so long as the relevant calculations of tuition paid subtract the amount paid by the Pell grant.

Raising the Pell Grant. Created in 1972, Pell grants are means-based tuition subsidies for poor college students. The usual economic justification of such grants is that some students might be prevented by liquidity constraints from making their optimal investments in college education. In their chapter in this volume, Cameron and Heckman show that few students appear to be prevented from attending college by short-term cash constraints. This suggests that capital markets for financing college are not as imperfect as sometimes thought and Pell grants have effectively eliminated many liquidity constraints. Although the Pell grant has risen by 16 percent in the past two years, the inflation-adjusted Pell grant is not particularly high relative to history. Moreover, since college costs have been increasing faster than inflation, the Pell grant as a percentage of average college costs has fallen since the program's inception.

As a marginal policy, there are no major disadvantages to raising the Pell grant. Some grants may be wasted by students who do not take college seriously, or may simply provide rent for colleges that exploit naïve students, but there is little reason to believe that the size of the increase will be sufficient to induce a significant increase in waste. The Pell grant does not encourage a general sense that college is an entitlement, since relatively few students are qualified to receive it. For the same reason (its limited use), it can have only minor effects on colleges' competitive behavior. The Pell grant does give some incentives to colleges to distort their tuitions in order to capture federal grant money. These incentives are weak for most colleges, however, because the Pell grants make up only a small percentage of their tuition revenue. Even two-year colleges, some of which get a substantial share of their revenue from Pell grants, would have a difficult time calculating the tuition increase that would capture the grant revenue without deterring students from enrolling. This is because the actual Pell grant a student receives depends on his individual circumstances as well as the college's tuition. Estimates based on the best empirical methods are preliminary (Li 1998), but they suggest that public two-year colleges increase their tuitions only slightly when the Pell grant increases—less than ten cents for every dollar of grant increase.

The Hope Credit. Clinton's initial vision of the Hope credit suggested that the thirteenth and fourteenth years of school could be made "universal" because the credit would make community college free or nearly free. The Hope credit's first problem arises precisely because of this vision. As discussed, community colleges are successful and cheap providers of remedial secondary school education, and empirical evidence suggests that a year of community college education earns a rate of return roughly equal to the rate of return earned on a year of baccalaureate education (Kane and Rouse 1995).[6] Unfortunately, the fact that community colleges provide a worthwhile service does not imply that it is good policy to make them nearly free and nearly universal. It is precisely because community college is *not* free and *not* universal that it succeeds with students who often have little to show for their secondary schooling. Also, if the thirteenth and fourteenth years of education were to become nearly free and universal, they would stop serving as an effective signal of job readiness, skills, and motivation; signals only work in equilibrium if there are sufficient cost hurdles to deter those who lack the attributes being signaled. If this were to occur, individuals would likely find it necessary to engage in a fifteenth year of education in order to signal the same degree of job readiness that they currently signal with only thirteen years. In summary, if the Hope credit were to succeed in making the thirteenth and fourteenth years of education nearly universal, it would probably do so at the cost of making college students less motivated and making two-year degrees less rewarded.

Another serious problem with the Hope credit is that it presents colleges, especially community colleges, with opportunities to raise tuition. Many colleges in the United States will have nearly every first- and second-year student receiving a tax credit of exactly $1,500, but tuition increases should be expected especially from two-year colleges because they often have local market power and they enroll only first- and second-year students—allowing them to raise tuition across-the-board, instead of through complex price discrimination. We cannot get a precise prediction for the effect of the Hope credit on tuition, but among two-year colleges that enroll students from a very local population, the information we have suggests that the estimated effect of the

---

6. This does not imply that two years of community college education are the equivalent of the first two years of a typical baccalaureate education. In fact, a small percentage of students who begin higher education in a community college make the successful transition to a baccalaureate program and ultimately complete a baccalaureate degree. Students who complete two years of community college earn a good rate of return because they pick up vocational skills and academic skills that they did not have when they graduated from high school (even if they should have had them). Community colleges also allow individuals to signal that they are motivated and job ready, distinguishing themselves within the large pool of high school graduates.

Pell grant on tuition (discussed above) would greatly understate the effect of the Hope credit.

The Tax Credit for Lifelong Learning. The tax credit for lifelong learning (TCLL) has some of the problems of the Hope credit, but it has them to a more modest degree. Because the TCLL gives a credit equal to only 20 percent of the tuition and fees that a family pays, students and their families are still responsible for the majority of tuition. Therefore, the TCLL is not likely to induce students to enroll in college for reasons that are more recreational than educational. Also, students will still have plenty of incentive to make enough effort to earn a private earnings return on a college education that is acquired at approximately a market rate of return.

A college might attempt to capture the TCLL by raising tuition by 20 percent of the first $5,000 ($10,000 after 2002). Colleges that have programs for upper-division undergraduates and graduate students, however, are more likely to be competing for mobile students. Among colleges that face a competitive market for students, any college that attempted to capture much of the TCLL without commensurate quality increases would lose students to its competition. Thus we should expect a portion of the TCLL to be reflected in tuition increases, but we should also expect commensurate increases in the package of services offered at most colleges that do not have local market power.

Penalty-Free Withdrawals from IRAs for College Expenses and Education IRAs (EIRAs). In comparison with regular savings accounts, IRA-EIRAs are a highly advantageous means of saving for college expenses. A good rule of thumb is that the number of before-tax dollars needed to achieve any given accumulation with a regular savings account is about 1.1 times the before-tax dollars needed with IRA-EIRAs. In short, the availability of IRA-EIRAs will substantially increase the average return to college saving. A family's *marginal* rate of return to college saving will increase if the amount [($2,000×no. of spouses) +($500×no. of children)] is larger than what its annual flow of new college saving would be in the absence of IRA-EIRAs. The maximum that could possibly be accumulated for a child's college expenses in IRA-EIRAs is about $109,000, in 1997 dollars. This accumulation assumes two parents who have only one child, who make the maximum contribution for each member of the family each year that the child is under the age of nineteen, and who earn a 3 percent real rate of return on their savings. But even an annual EIRA contribution as small as $200 would provide a student with about $4,800 in 1997 dollars.

The most important benefit of the IRA-EIRA is that by encouraging families to put savings into accounts dedicated to college expenses, it will make families think about college education earlier and with greater commitment. It appears that there is an educational advantage to early commitment. Students make more optimal college decisions and more effort in secondary school when they are interested early on in preparing to attend college. As Owen (1995) notes, much of students' failure to prepare well for college while in secondary school comes from the "remoteness" of the college choice decision. By establishing a college savings account, a student will think more concretely about the return to college education.

IRA-EIRAs have few, if any, dangers for the higher education sector because they will mainly help people to afford the college education in which they truly want to invest. The subsidy is so specific to each individual's savings decisions that IRA-EIRAs are unlikely to generate tuition increases—although a reduction in need-based aid may counteract the subsidy for students in selective colleges.

Tax Deductions for Interest Paid on Student Loans. Unfortunately, IRA-EIRAs generate more optimal human capital investments only for students whose parents are able or willing to save for college expenses. For students who do not receive a sufficient boost to their incentives through this channel, the 1998 budget contained a deduction for interest paid on student loans. In 1998, an individual could deduct from his taxable income up to $1,000 of interest that he paid during the year. By 2001, the maximum deduction will have risen to $2,500. The deduction is above the line—that is, an individual need not itemize to take the deduction. If the deduction is taken, then the effective interest rate is $i \times (1 - \tau)$, where i is the statutory rate and τ is the income tax rate that applies to the borrower.

The maximum 1998 deduction of $1,000 is sufficiently small that the *marginal* rate of interest will not change for about one-fifth of students who have outstanding loans. It is important to remember that the maximum deduction is per household, not per student. Thus, the deductibility of interest paid on student loans will be a substantially more powerful policy in 2002, at which time the maximum deduction will be $2,500.

The major economic benefit of the tax deduction is that it can make human capital investments more optimal by subsidizing the cost of borrowing to finance such investments. Market failures for investments in human capital tend to make students require a rate of return to investments in human capital that is excessive relative to that which is socially optimal. The main causes of failure in the market for student loans is that a student's investment in his human capital is noncollateralizable and nondiversifiable. Being risk averse, students require a rate of return on the investment that is higher than the average rate of return to other economic investments. The deductibility of interest on student loans reduces students' required rate of return and, thus, is likely to move human capital investment toward the social optimum.

Unfortunately, the deductibility of interest on student loans discourages college savings because it lowers the price of financing through loans relative to financing through saving. For the same reason that the policy "insures" students against the accident of having parents who are unable or unwilling to save, the policy discourages saving. Apart from this disadvantage, the student loan interest deduction has few dangers for the higher education sector because, like the IRA-EIRA, it mainly addresses capital market failures for students who already want to invest in college education.

Note the general difference between (1) the tax credits and (2) the IRA-EIRA and student loan interest deduction. The two latter policies can be justified because they address obvious failures in the capital market for human capital investment. Moreover, the two latter *intervene in the capital market*—by raising the return to savings for college investments and lowering the cost of borrowing for college investments. The subsidy received is a function of a student's use of the capital market. In contrast, the tax credits are functions of the tuition a student pays. As a result, the tax credits are more likely to provoke tuition increases and must be justified by the argument that higher education is a public good—an argument easier to make for elementary and secondary schooling, of course.

Toward the Most Effective Higher Education Policy

The differing market structure of the primary-secondary and higher education sectors accounts for the fact that American colleges and universities are significantly more successful and efficient at producing education than are elementary and secondary schools. This is one reason why the higher education sector is the logical focus for federal policy that seeks to make the best use of tax money. Another reason is that federal money has more leverage in higher education than in elementary and secondary education. In sum, the disproportionate weight traditionally given to higher education in federal budgets seems appropriate.

Ultimately, federal policy should attempt to help the higher education sector do more than educate and remediate—that is, provide education to those whose secondary schooling is inadequate. It should make the higher education sector a lever that puts pressure on elementary and secondary schools to perform. This can be done by allowing students to use their secondary school money for college courses, as is done in Minnesota. Also, colleges can be rewarded for setting tougher curricular and achievement standards, since these standards set an example for secondary schools.

References

Breneman, D. 1998. "The Extent and Cost of Remediation in Higher Education." In *Brookings Papers in Education Policy,* edited by Diane Ravitch. Washington, D.C.: Brookings Institution.

Cameron, S., and J. Heckman. 1997. Paper presented at the American Enterprise Institute.

Clotfelter, C. 1996. *Buying the Best: Cost Escalation in Elite Higher Education.* Princeton: Princeton University Press.

Dick, A., and A. Edlin. Forthcoming. "The Implicit Taxes from College Financial Aid." *Journal of Public Economics.*

Edlin, A. 1993. "Is College Financial Aid Equitable and Efficient?" *Journal of Economic Perspectives,* pp. 143–58.

Ehrenberg, R., and S. Murphy. 1993. "What Price Diversity? The Death of Need Based Financial Aid at Selective Private Colleges and Universities." Typescript of an article that was published (shortened) in *Change.*

Feldstein, M. 1995. "College Scholarship Rules and Private Saving." *American Economic Review,* pp. 552–66.

Goldin, Claudia. 1998. "America's Graduation from High School: The Evolution and Spread of Secondary Schooling in the Twentieth Century." *Journal of Economic History* 58 (2) (June): 345–74.

Hoxby, C. 1997a. "How the Changing Market Structure of American College Education Explains Tuition." NBER Working Paper. Cambridge, Mass.: National Bureau of Economic Research.

———. 1997b. "The Changing Market Structure of U.S. Higher Education: 1920 to the Present." NBER Working Paper. Cambridge, Mass.: National Bureau of Economic Research.

Kane, T. 1997. "Beyond Tax Relief: Long-Term Challenges in Financing Higher Education." *National Tax Journal,* pp. 335–49.

Kane, T., and C. Rouse. 1995. "Labor Market Returns to Two- and Four-Year College." *American Economic Review.*

Kim, Taejong. 1997. "College Financial Aid and Family Saving." Ph.D. diss., MIT.

Lalonde, R., L. Jacobson, and D. Sullivan. 1997. "The Returns from Community College Schooling for Displaced Workers." NBER Working Paper. Cambridge, Mass.: National Bureau of Economic Research.

Li, Judith. 1998. "Do Increases in the Pell Grant Cause Colleges To Raise Tuition? A Test of the Bennett Hypothesis." Ph.D. diss., Harvard University.

Murnane, R., J. Willett, and F. Levy. 1995. "The Increasing Importance of Cognitive Skills in Wage Determination." *Review of Economics and Statistics*, pp. 251–66.

National Center for Education Statistics. 1996. "Postsecondary Education." In *Digest of Educational Statistics, 1996*, Chap. 3. Washington, D.C.: Government Printing Office.

Owen, J. 1995. *Why Our Kids Don't Study: An Economist's Perspective.* Baltimore: Johns Hopkins University Press.

Rothschild, M., and L. White. 1995. "The Analytics of the Pricing of Higher Education and Other Services in Which the Customers Are Inputs." *Journal of Political Economy*, pp. 573–86.

Thaler, R. 1991. "Anomalies: The Endowment Effect, Loss Aversion, and Status Quo Bias." *Journal of Economic Perspectives*, pp. 193–206.

Turner, S. 1997. "Does Federal Aid Affect College Costs? Evidence from the Pell Program." Typescript, Curry School of Education, University of Virginia.

U.S. Department of Education, National Center for Education Statistics. 1996. *Digest of Educational Statistics.* Washington, D.C.: Government Printing Office.

4

Reforming Public Subsidies for Higher Education

Thomas J. Kane

That the bottom has fallen out of the market for high school graduates is well known now. The gap in earnings between high school and college graduates has widened dramatically. It is less well known, however, that families and youths have been busily responding: between 1980 and 1995, the proportion of eighteen- to twenty-four-year-olds enrolled in college increased by one-third (DoE 1996, 189, t. 182). The number of associate, bachelor's, and master's degrees awarded also increased by roughly one-third.[1] With the current surge in college enrollment, policy makers no longer can simply spread the word that college is more important than it was. Rather, the challenge is to find a way to pay for college for the growing numbers of youths who are seeking to enter. In this chapter, I present the scope of the challenge and current financial aid policies, and conclude with suggestions for reform.

Enrollment by Test Scores and Family Income

Figure 4–1 reports the proportion of eighteen- to twenty-four-year-old youths enrolled in college as well as the wage ratio between college and high school graduates with one to five years of experience. During the 1970s, when the gap in earnings between high school and college graduates was shrinking, college enrollment rates stagnated. Soon

Part of this chapter is drawn from the author's article in the June 1997 *National Tax Journal* and from a book, *The Price of Admission: Rethinking How Americans Pay for College,* forthcoming from the Brookings Institution. The author acknowledges the generous support of the Andrew W. Mellon Foundation.

1. This rise in degrees earned is particularly noteworthy given the decline in the size of the college age cohort over the period (DoE 1996, 253, t. 239).

FIGURE 4–1
COLLEGE ENROLLMENT RATES AND COLLEGE WAGE PREMIUMS,
1967–1995

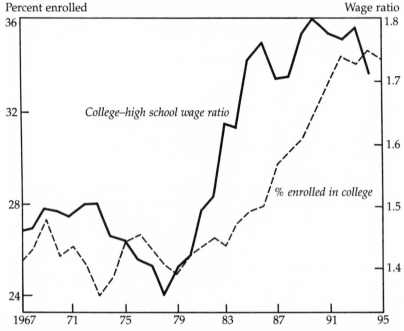

SOURCE: The wage ratios for those with one to five years of potential experience were provided by Kevin Murphy. The proportion of eighteen- to twenty-four-year-olds enrolled in college was estimated from the October Current Population Survey data (DOE 1996, 189, t. 182).

after the college–high school earnings differential began to widen late in that decade, college enrollment rates began rising. This trend continued throughout the 1980s and early 1990s. Although both series remained high in 1994, the rise in college enrollment has tapered off in recent years as the rise in the payoff to college has slowed.

While enrollment rates have generally been rising, however, low-income students seem to have fallen behind. Figure 4–2 compares the proportion of students entering a four-year college within two years of high school graduation by family income level for the high school classes of 1982 and 1992. The proportion of high school students entering college has increased. But the increases been particularly large among those from families with incomes above $50,000. Entry rates did not rise similarly for those with incomes below $12,000.

Given the preexisting gap in college entry by family income, the

FIGURE 4-2

PROPORTION OF HIGH SCHOOL CLASSES OF 1982 AND 1992 ENTERING A
FOUR-YEAR COLLEGE, BY FAMILY INCOME
(in 1998 dollars)

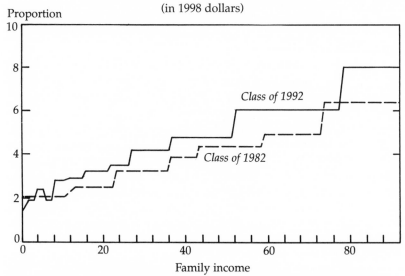

SOURCE: The estimates in figure 4–2 are based on the author's tabulation of the High School and Beyond Survey of those with high school diplomas from the class of 1982 and the National Education Longitudinal Study of those graduating from high school in 1992.

dramatic rise in the college–high school wage premium would have meant a widening gap in earnings prospects for youths from high- and low-income families. Yet, even if the gaps in college enrollment by family income were held constant, a rise in the value of an advantage, such as a college education, disproportionately enjoyed by more privileged youths means that higher-income youths gained relative to low-income youths. A widening gap in college enrollment rates merely exacerbates that trend. In other words, if all else were held constant, parental income may have become an even stronger predictor of children's expected earnings than in the past.[2]

The Current Approach to Financing

State, local, and federal governments primarily employ two types of subsidies to help families pay for higher education. First, and by far

2. However, a rise in within-education-group earnings inequality may have offset somewhat the correlation between parental means and youths' means.

the largest historically, are the direct appropriations from state and local governments to public postsecondary institutions. In 1993–1994, state and local governments appropriated $45 billion in subsidies to public institutions of higher education; the bulk of the funding was used to keep tuition charges low for in-state students. Less than 10 percent of the state spending was provided in the form of means-tested grants (DoE 1996, 334).

These direct state appropriations to public colleges and universities are often attacked as regressive. Hansen and Weisbrod (1969), for example, touched off a lively debate nearly three decades ago by pointing out that those from middle- and higher-income families were more likely to attend any college than low-income youths and much more likely to attend the elite public four-year institutions that received a large share of such subsidies.[3] (See the relationship between college attendance and income in figure 4–2.) Critics, most notably Pechman (1970), responded that the net progressivity of such subsidies depended not only on the income distribution of public college students but also on the marginal source of revenue used to pay for public higher education. Pechman argued that if state income taxes were the marginal source of revenue, then, on net, public subsidies to higher education may still be equitably distributed since higher-income families pay a disproportionate share of public subsidies for higher education as taxpayers. An obvious obstacle to resolving the question is the difficulty in identifying the marginal source of revenue for higher education.

The second largest form of public subsidy to higher education is the means-tested grant and loan programs to help families pay for college. The largest of these is the federal Pell grant program, currently distributing approximately $6 billion per year in grants to low-income youths and adults. Most states also have their own grant programs to supplement the Pell grants, although total spending on state need-based grant programs was roughly one-half the size of the Pell grant spending. In addition, the federal government spends several billion dollars per year to pay the interest on loans for students in school and to pay off defaulted loans.

With the exception of the defaulted loans, most of this aid is distributed according to a backward-looking assessment of a student's ability to pay. For dependent undergraduates (defined as those who are not married, under age twenty-four, with no military experience and no dependents), eligibility for aid is based not only on their own

---

3. Between 1970 and 1977, the *Journal of Human Resources* published at least seven separate responses to an article by Hansen and Weisbrod in that journal.

income and assets but also on family income and financial assets. Such backward-looking means testing implicitly taxes income and savings by providing less aid to those with higher incomes and assets. Because only a single year of income (the previous tax year) is considered and because the implicit marginal levy on savings (5.6 percent) is repeated each year a child is in school, these marginal tax rates on assets (and therefore on savings) have often been quite large.[4] Edlin (1993) and Feldstein (1995) estimated that the marginal tax on savings can reach nearly 50 percent for those with children in college over a span of eight years.[5]

Subsequent work has suggested that these estimated tax rates may be overstated somewhat for several reasons. First, the marginal tax rate for financial aid is zero for those whose incomes are already too high to qualify for financial aid. Three-quarters of four-year college students attend public four-year universities, which have an average annual tuition of roughly $3,000. Relatively few of those with financial assets larger than the asset protection allowances would be qualifying for any aid at these low-cost institutions. Second, the tax-rate calculations above assumed that any difference between the cost of attendance and the expected family contribution was being met. Yet, as Dick and Edlin (1996) report, the average college does not meet students' full financial need. Rather than a 50 percent tax on savings, Dick and Edlin estimated a marginal asset levy of 8–26 percent and marginal income taxes of 2–16 percent for those attending the average-priced college. Finally, housing assets were excluded from the federal financial aid formula during the last reauthorization of the Higher Education Act in 1992, although many colleges continue to consider parental assets when distributing their own financial aid resources.

Still, the implicit tax rates on parental savings and income, though possibly overstated in the early work of Edlin and Feldstein, are bound to become increasingly important. The cost of providing a year of college education (as opposed to the current tuition charge), even at a public four-year institution, is roughly $12,000 and rising. To keep out-of-pocket costs low for low-income youths but to have middle- and higher-income youths paying closer to the cost of attendance, the tax rates will be unavoidably steep. One need only understand the basic rules of geometry to see this. If, for instance, youths with family in-

---

4. For more on implicit tax rates in financial aid formulas, see Edlin (1993), Feldstein (1995), and Dick and Edlin (1996).

5. The average tax rates on savings remain low, however, given asset protection allowances of $36,000 for married parents at age forty-five, ranging up to $66,000 for parents sixty-five and older.

comes below $20,000 were to pay no net tuition and those with incomes above $50,000 were to pay full cost, "taking away" a $12,000 benefit over a $30,000 income range would require a marginal tax rate of more than one-third. When added to existing state and federal income taxes, this would imply a high tax rate indeed. State governments have moderated such marginal tax rates by providing across-the-board subsidies to students attending public institutions to keep tuition low relative to the actual cost of providing the education. As argued below, however, such a system becomes expensive when an increasing number of youths attend college and it would be reasonable to expect tuition levels to rise.

Sources of Rising College Tuition. College tuition has risen sharply over the past decade and a half. Between 1980 and 1995, the average tuition (including required fees) at public and private four-year colleges grew by 91 percent and 83 percent, respectively, even after taking account of general changes in consumer prices (DoE 1996, 320, t. 309). The magnitude of such increases led Congress and the president to take the unprecedented step of creating a national commission to look into the issue, the National Commission on the Cost of Higher Education (1998).

When discussing the phenomenon of rising tuition bills, however, one must be careful to distinguish between the terms *tuition* and *cost.* At public colleges and universities, tuition increases have far outstripped underlying increases in costs per student. Between 1980 and 1995, real public tuition levels rose by 91 and 72 percent, respectively, at public four-year and two-year institutions—even though the educational costs per student (including faculty salaries, library costs, student support services) rose by just 20 percent.[6] In other words, the price that students pay has been rising much more quickly than the actual costs per student at public colleges and universities. States—which have traditionally paid a large share of the costs with direct subsidies to institutions—have been compelled by other demands on their budgets to cut their subsidies per student and to raise the share of costs paid by students and their families. This decline in the share of costs covered by state subsidies—as opposed to a sharp increase in costs themselves—accounts for most of the increase in tuition at public institutions, which enroll three-quarters of four-year college students. Thus, the tuition hikes have had just as much to do with the rise in public college enrollment and the fiscal decisions of state legislatures as with an increased educational expenditure per student.

---

6. These figures include the costs of instruction, administration, student ser-

Real cost inflation—as opposed to tuition inflation—has been much more striking, however, at private institutions. First, while sticker prices increased by roughly the same magnitude as at public institutions (83 percent), the price paid by the average student rose by only half that rate, after taking account of offsetting increases in institutional grant aid. With the decline in federal need-based grant aid discussed below, private universities have increasingly used the tuition paid by some to keep costs down for others. Even though the tuition increases overstate the actual rise in average net tuition increases, however, cost increases were larger at private four-year universities than at public universities. Costs per student rose by approximately the same amount as net tuition paid per student—more than 40 percent. Despite a careful analysis by Clotfelter (1996), the source of this increase in costs at private institutions is not well understood. But we should keep the issue of cost escalation in perspective and recognize that private institutions enroll only 25 percent of all four-year college students. The forces driving most families' difficulty in paying for college is a result of state budget politics and the tuition levels established at public universities, as opposed to the managerial acumen of college administrators.

Demographics of the Baby Boomlet. Even if public institutions succeed in holding the line on cost increases, the pressure to raise the levels of tuition at public institutions is likely to build. The size of the college-age population—which has declined by 15 percent since 1980 and partially relieved the cost pressures from rising college enrollment rates—is projected to rise by one-fifth over the next fifteen years (BoC 1995, 17, t. 17). As portrayed in figure 4–3, the renewed expansion of the college-age population is expected to be even more rapid in the West (particularly California), where the population of fifteen- to twenty-four-year-olds is projected to increase by twice the national rate (Callan and Finney 1993). If future cohorts of college-age youths attempt to maintain the same high college-entry rates as the smaller cohorts today—and the labor market conditions that have driven such rates upward show no sign of abating—public budgets for higher education are likely to be stretched thin. Therefore, because of these demographics, families may be paying an even higher proportion of the costs, even if college administrators are more successful in limiting cost increases.

---

vices, libraries, and the operation and maintenance of colleges physical plants, but exclude expenditures on scholarships. Figures were adjusted for increases in consumer prices (DoE 1996, 352–53, t. 339–340).

FIGURE 4–3
PROJECTED GROWTH IN FIFTEEN- TO TWENTY-FOUR-YEAR-OLD
POPULATION, 1995–2015

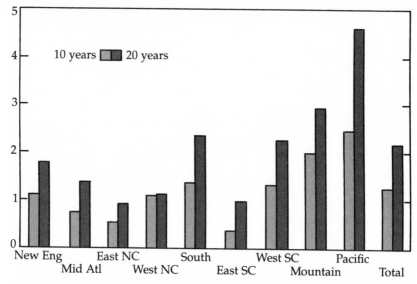

SOURCE: Campbell (1994).

Effects of College Pricing Policies on Enrollment

As portrayed in figure 4–2, college-entry rates rise with family income. Such differences are often implicitly attributed to differences in families' abilities to self-finance a college education. The causes of this widely noted empirical regularity, however, are not well understood. As Cameron and Heckman (1997) point out, rather than simply mirroring differences in ability to pay, such differences may reflect differences in academic preparation, in access to information about college, or in the rate of time preference or taste for education of a family. Youths from higher-income families may be more likely to go to college not only because their parents can afford it, but also because they are better prepared to take advantage of a college education, or because they value that education more highly. Most empirical treatments of the question do not attempt to sort out the various ways in which family background might affect educational attainment.

Past research employed one of two sources of variation in college pricing policies to identify the importance of such policies to enrollment decisions.[7] First, many researchers have used cross-sectional variation in the public tuition charges to study the importance of college costs. Given the importance of state subsidies to higher education, a convenient source of variation in college costs is the differences by state in tuition charged at public two-year and four-year institutions.[8] A second source of variation is the change over time in federal financial aid policies. Both sets of results are discussed below.

Cross-Sectional Analysis. Cross-sectional analyses generally report that college enrollment rates are lower in states with higher average tuition charges for public higher education, particularly in states with high tuition at two-year institutions. Note that this sort of evidence is quite different from that which state legislators and governors would observe in their own states: college enrollment rates were rising as tuition was rising. However, this need not have meant that demand curves slope up, since other things were changing over time, such as the earnings differentials enjoyed by college graduates. Although not all youths attend public institutions, the implicit model in such cross-sectional analyses is that for those on the margin of attending college, it is the tuition at a public institution that counts. Moreover, the negative relationship between state tuition levels and enrollment is particularly striking for low-income youths in these states. In table 4–1, I report an example of such an analysis using data from the High School and Beyond Survey of the class of 1982. (See Kane 1995a for similar results with alternative data sets.) Table 4–1 reports the difference in the probability of postsecondary school enrollment within four years after the sophomore year in high school. The estimates were generated with a probit specification, and the differences in the likelihood of admission were evaluated at the sample mean. Although not all derivatives are reported (in the interest of space), each specification included measures of family income, parental education, state unemployment rate, and student test scores and high school grades in academic subjects. (Standard errors were calculated appropriately, in recognition of the use of group-level regressors.)

Column 1 evaluates the relative importance of differences in state two-year and four-year tuition. A difference of $1,000 (in 1991 dollars) in tuition at a public two-year institution was associated with a 17 percentage point difference in likelihood of admission. (The mean tuition

---

7. For a more complete review of the literature on the price elasticity of demand for higher education, see Leslie and Brinkman (1988).

8. For examples of such studies, see Kane (1994), Kane (1995a), and Cameron and Heckman (1998).

TABLE 4–1
PROBABILITY OF POSTSECONDARY ENROLLMENT BY STATE TUITION,
NEED-BASED GRANT SPENDING, AND UNEMPLOYMENT RATE
FOR THE CLASS OF 1982

	Full Sample	By Quartile of SES			
		Bottom	2nd	3rd	Top
Public 2-year tuition in state (/$1,000)	−.177 (.046)	−.197 (.064)	−.121 (.050)	−.156 (.030)	−.005 (.025)
Public 4-year tuition in state (/$1,000)	.021 (.050)				
State grants per capita ($100/ person aged 15–24)	.113 (.027)	.147 (.065)	.070 (.039)	.073 (.021)	.005 (.014)
State unemployment rate (/10)	−.057 (.112)	−.216 (.184)	.050 (.128)	−.103 (.093)	.613 (.879)
Sample size	9,654	2,212	2,154	2,108	2,300
Mean postsecondary enrollment rate	.644	.437	.594	.711	.875

NOTE: The above were estimated using a probit specification with a sample of 9,654 high school sophomores from 1980. The dependent variable was any reported postsecondary school enrollment by 1984. The tuition and financial aid measures represent the average for the state in which a student attended high school. Also included in each specification were eight dummy variables for high school census division, eight for family income category, five for parental education category, test score composite in 1982, and grade point average on academic subjects in high school. SES is a composite measure of family income, parental education, and parental occupation. Robust standard errors (reported in parentheses) were calculated while allowing the errors to be correlated among those living in the same state.
SOURCE: High School and Beyond Survey, Class of 1982.

at a public two-year institution in 1982 was $809.) This is quite a large effect, given the mean postsecondary entry rate of 62 percent. After controlling for the state's public two-year tuition, there was little difference in college enrollment associated with public four-year tuition levels. These are precisely the expected results if the person on the margin of getting any postsecondary training is primarily concerned with a community college. Greater state spending on need-based grants for college was also associated with higher postsecondary entry rates. A difference of $100 in state need-based grant spending per person aged fifteen to twenty-four was associated with an 11 percentage point difference in postsecondary entry. (The mean spending per capita on such programs was $48 per person aged fifteen to twenty-four.)

The remaining columns in table 4–1 report the results estimated separately by the quartile for socioeconomic status (SES), a composite measure of family income and parental education reported by the High School and Beyond Survey. (Given the suspected poor quality of the student-reported family income data, the SES measure may be a better proxy for family income and wealth.) The percentage point differences in college enrollment rates associated with differences in tuition are larger for the lower SES quartiles. These differences are even greater in percentage terms, given the lower entry rates of those in the lower quartiles. Moreover, the differences in postsecondary entry rates associated with differences in state spending on need-based grant programs are also larger for the lower SES quartiles. Both results are consistent with a model in which liquidity constraints are an important source of the differences in college entry rates by family income.

Time Series Evidence. The time series evidence on the effectiveness of federal financial aid programs has not been nearly as robust as the cross-sectional estimates. In 1973, the federal Pell grant program was established to provide grants to low-income youths. Because the program affected only low-income youths, enrollment rates for low-income youths might have been expected to increase disproportionately.[9] In a provocative paper published more than a decade ago, Hansen (1983) found little growth in enrollment by low-income youths during the 1970s. But McPherson and Schapiro (1991) identified two weaknesses in Hansen's approach, which are corrected here. Hansen used only two years of data on either side of the policy change; this presumably weakened the power of his test. Second, because of pooling males and females, the program effect estimated by Hansen was contaminated by any change in college-going behavior by males at the end of the Vietnam War.

To address both concerns, table 4–2 reports the program effect only for women and pools eight years of data. The data from the October CPS are broken into two periods: 1970–1972 (before the Pell grant program) and 1973–1977 (after the program began). The growth in enrollment rates for those from families in the lowest-income quartile (most of whom would have been eligible for Pell grants) is then compared with the trend in enrollment rates for those from the top three

---

9. Amendments in 1978 would have opened the program to middle-class students. For a description of these changes, see Manski and Wise (1983).

TABLE 4–2
CHANGES IN COLLEGE ENROLLMENT RATES OF DEPENDENT EIGHTEEN-
TO NINETEEN-YEAR-OLD FEMALES, BY FAMILY-INCOME QUARTILE,
1970–72 TO 1973–77

	Any College Enrollment		Private College Enrollment		Public 2-Year College Enrollment	
	(1)	(2)	(3)	(4)	(5)	(6)
Black, non-Hispanic (relative to white, non-Hispanic)	−.027 (.023)	.044 (.020)	.000 (.013)	.034 (.013)	−.029 (.014)	.000 (.013)
After Pell grants (1973–77) (relative to 1970–72)	.025 (.010)	−.008 (.010)	.022 (.006)	−.003 (.005)	−.009 (.007)	−.010 (.007)
Black after Pell grants	.027 (.028)	−.015 (.025)	−.010 (.016)	−.027 (.015)	.005 (.018)	.012 (.017)
Lowest-income quartile after Pell grants	−.026 (.023)	.005 (.022)	−.028 (.013)	−.002 (.009)	.034 (.015)	.024 (.015)
Family background included?	No	Yes	No	Yes	No	Yes
N	12,163	12,163	12,163	12,163	12,163	12,163

NOTE: The above were estimated within a linear probability framework. Included in all equations were dummy variables for income quartiles, region,
and a constant term. Family background measures included ten dummy variables for parents' education and homeownership.
SOURCE: DoE (1996).

quartiles. Three different dependent variables are used: total college
enrollment rates, enrollment rates in private universities, and enrollment rates in public two-year institutions. Total college enrollment
rates grew 2.6 percentage points more *slowly* for the lowest-income
quartile over the period (although this difference was not significantly
different from zero). Further, private college enrollment grew by 2.8
percentage points *less* for low-income youth over the period when the
Pell grant program was established. Only enrollment for public two-
year colleges seemed to grow more quickly for low-income youths.
(Total college enrollment rates, however, did not increase more rapidly:
there may have been some relative shifts in enrollment among different
types of colleges.) As reported in columns 2, 4, and 6, adding family

background measures such as parental education and homeownership has little effect on the results.[10]

As confirmed by the heated reaction to Hansen's original paper, such evidence certainly challenges the belief that grant programs open the doors to college for many low-income youths. It is not simply that a small treatment effect of Pell grants was expected: the maximum Pell grant in 1975 was $3,544 (1991$). On the basis of the cross-sectional estimates, we would have expected low-income youths receiving the maximum grant to have increased enrollment rates by more than 20 percentage points.

Possible Resolutions. The empirical evidence on college cost and college entry, therefore, leaves us in a bit of a quandary. On one hand, cross-sectional differences in state tuition and financial aid policies have consistently been found to be associated with large differences in college entry rates for students in different states. On the other hand, the time series evidence following the establishment of student aid programs in the mid-1970s reveals no disproportionate increase in college enrollment for low-income students.

At least two hypotheses would reconcile these results. First, the cross-sectional impacts are overstated because of unobserved state effects; that is, "low-tuition" states differ systematically from other states. One low-tuition state, California, for instance, encourages college enrollment in another way, by building a number of community colleges around the state. Attempts by Kane (1994), Kane (1995a), and Cameron and Heckman (1998) to identify the importance of state fixed-effects have yielded inconclusive results, possibly because of the paucity of data with which to study within-state variation in tuition. Additional work, focusing on the large tuition increases in some states during the late 1980s and early 1990s, may yet shed some light on this

---

10. Not all time series evidence yields similarly small estimates of the effect of cost on enrollment. McPherson and Schapiro (1991), for instance, used national aggregate time series data on enrollment rates of low-income white students and found that enrollment rates declined by roughly 6 points for every $1,000 increase in net direct costs. Though the estimate is quite similar to that reported in cross-sectional work, it is based primarily on the common timing of a decline in enrollment rates for low-income youths in the early 1980s and an increase in state tuition levels. Many other things, however, were changing over the same period. Both trends, for instance, coincided with a serious recession. With only time variation in costs and enrollment rates, it is impossible to distinguish the effect of tuition increases from other unmeasured changes that may have changed over time and affected the national market for a college education.

issue. A second possible reconciliation argues that the marginal student may simply have been unaware of the availability of Pell grants in the first few years of the program. Orfield (1992) cited several studies suggesting that low-income families may not have been aware of eligibility rules and procedures. A 1975 study in New Jersey, for example, suggested that a quarter of low-income college students had not even applied for aid, even though many would have qualified for a Pell grant (New Jersey Commission on Financing Postsecondary Education 1975). The actual impacts of Pell grants on student enrollments may be larger today as awareness of program rules and application processes has grown.

Thus far, empirical research has had to rely almost solely on the "natural experiments" available in observational data. Unfortunately, those results have often been inconsistent. Given the size of the state and federal investment, federal funding for a random-assignment evaluation of alternative approaches—varying the monetary value of the grants available as well as varying the amount of counseling and information provided—may well be a worthwhile investment.[11]

Recent Tax Expenditures

In August 1997, Congress and the president reached agreement on a number of new tax expenditures to help families pay for higher education. First, families with students in their first two years of college will receive a tax credit of up to $1,500 per student for out-of-pocket tuition expenses. This credit, designated as the Hope tax credit, will be given for 100 percent of tuition expenses (less any federal, state, or private grant aid) up to $1,000 and 50 percent of any remaining expenses up to $2,000. Room and board expenses will not count for the credit. Eligibility for the credit will be phased out for families with incomes between $80,000 and $100,000 and for single filers with income between $40,000 and $50,000.

Second, those taking classes beyond their first two years of college will be eligible to receive a 20 percent credit on the first $5,000 of out-of-pocket tuition expenses. The maximum, which will be raised to $10,000 in 2003, will apply to each taxpaying unit, not to each student. Eligibility limits will be the same as for the Hope tax credit.

Third, parents will be able to withdraw funds from existing individual retirement accounts to pay for tuition or room and board. Such withdrawals will not be subject to the usual 10 percent penalty. Unless

---

11. For more details on the savings incentives implicit in the Taxpayer Relief Act of 1997, see Kane (1998).

the account holder is over age fifty-nine, however, any capital gains will still be taxable.

Fourth, a child under the age of eighteen can have $500 per year deposited in his behalf to help pay for future tuition and room and board expenses. Any single taxpayer with an income less than $95,000 and joint-filing taxpayers with incomes less than $100,000 can make such contributions. Unlike withdrawals from other IRAs, the capital gains on the new education IRAs will not be taxable up to the cost of tuition and room and board.

Fifth, parents or students will be able to deduct up to $1,000 in interest on loans used to pay for education expenses. This limit will be raised in $500 increments to $2,500 by the year 2001. Eligibility for the deduction will be limited to individuals with incomes less than $40,000 and to joint filers with incomes less than $60,000.

Sixth, student loans provided by tax-exempt organizations, such as universities or state governments, will now be forgiven with no tax liability for the beneficiary as long as the person is working for a tax-exempt organization or governmental unit in an underserved occupation or geographic area. In the past, graduates would have had to pay federal income tax on loans that were forgiven, with the exception of some special federal loan programs.

Finally, participants in state-run prepaid tuition plans will receive a relatively small incremental benefit. Previously, funds could be withdrawn to pay for the cost of tuition. Now, such funds can also be used to pay for room and board. Participants will still pay a tax on any capital gains at withdrawal. The primary tax advantage offered such plans—that no tax is paid on the income of such plans until withdrawal—will remain in place.

Evaluation of Initiatives. The final legislation improved on the initial proposal from the administration in a number of ways. (In fact, the administration itself supported many improvements.) Congress, for instance, wisely dropped the requirement that students maintain a B average to qualify for the tax credit. In addition to the administrative difficulties in asking the Internal Revenue Service to confirm student transcripts, the hoped-for behavioral benefits were not obvious. Indeed, given the likelihood of grade inflation and grade-conscious coursework choices by risk-averse students, the behavioral response may even have been counterproductive. A number of difficulties, however, remain.

First, the tax benefits are not well targeted. Figure 4–2 reported that many families were already responding to labor market developments by enrolling in college at higher rates. Low-income families are the only group that seems to be lagging. The new tax expenditures, however, offer low-income families little. Because neither tax credit is refundable, families must have substantial federal tax liability to qualify for the credit. Moreover, because only out-of-pocket expenses are counted—tuition minus any grants received—the proposal essentially reduces the progressivity of existing means-tested formulas since it was analogous to a cut in the benefit reduction rate on income in the financial aid formula. The allowance of early withdrawals from existing IRAs to pay for educational expenses is a windfall for those with already substantial IRA assets. The estimated cost of these new tax expenditures is $41 billion over five years—making them roughly the same magnitude as the primary federal means-tested grant program—and virtually all of it goes to middle- and higher-income families.

Second, because the $1,500 tax credit provides a 100 percent credit on the first $1,000 in out-of-pocket expenses and effectively does not require any copayment on expenses up to $1,000, it encourages eligible institutions to offer leisure-oriented courses for college credit to taxpayers qualifying for the subsidy. As long as such courses cost less than $1,000 and could superficially qualify for degree credits, those attending such courses will be fully reimbursed. Colleges, for instance, could offer $1,000 whale-watching tours to taxpayers as long as they granted them half-time credit toward a marine biology degree. Since the IRS cannot be expected to monitor course content, the tax credit is likely to fund a large number of frivolous adult education courses.

Third, those institutions with tuition less than $5,000 have a strong incentive to relabel room and board charges as tuition charges to qualify for the tax credit and thereby raise the estimated cost of the proposal. Under previous law, colleges had no incentive to shift room and board expenses into tuition charges since they were treated equivalently in the student aid formulas. Those colleges with current tuition charges below $5,000 (primarily public institutions), however, will be tempted to charge on-campus students "tuition" for access to dormitory study halls and so forth. A fifth of the 6 million students at public four-year colleges live on campus and pay room and board charges averaging roughly $4,000. This would be less of a concern at private institutions since their tuition is generally above $5,000.

Prospects for Tuition Inflation. Despite the fears of some of the plan's critics (and perhaps even contrary to the secret hopes of some of the plan's supporters in the higher education community), the tax expenditure legislation is unlikely to lead to rampant tuition inflation. Although the plan may provide welcome tax relief to families, it will have scant effect on the marginal cost to families when an institution raises tuition. The few institutions with tuition below $1,000 will have a clear incentive to raise their tuition since students in families with sufficient taxable income would be paying nothing on the margin. Likewise, those with tuition between $1,000 and $2,000 will be receiving 50 percent tax subsidies to cover the cost. Those with out-of-pocket tuition costs above $2,000, however, will be receiving at most 20 percent on the margin for tuition increases up to $5,000. (Indeed, first- and second-year students at such institutions will be paying 100 percent of any tuition increase since they would be expected to be taking the Hope tax credit rather than the other type of credit.) Above $5,000, families would be paying 100 percent of any tuition increase. Facing prospects of declining enrollments or, at public institutions, the political resistance of angry parents, colleges may properly hesitate to raise tuition.

The primary impact of the tax expenditures will be an income effect rather than a price effect—as if the federal government were sending families a tax refund unrelated to how much more they spend on college. Families will spend some of these tax savings on higher education but will likely spend most on other consumption, such as a summer vacation or new furniture. Colleges may capture a portion of the benefit when families choose to consume more education with their tax windfall, particularly those colleges with considerable market power. But, in the end, relatively little of the tax relief will likely convert into faculty salaries, dormitories, and libraries.

An Alternative Approach to Reform

The higher education tax expenditures of 1997 provide welcome tax relief for middle-income families struggling to pay tuition bills. While these families may be content to have the tax relief, however, the proposal does nothing to solve some structural weaknesses in our current system for financing college. Given the economic and demographic forces pushing college enrollment rates up, the real challenge over the next decade will be to design a financial aid system that does not discourage family earnings or savings, that encourages students to make the most of the value of the resources at their disposal, and that allows students from all family backgrounds to make worthwhile investments in college. Congress could consider the following list of more ambitious reforms.

First, the Department of Education should fund demonstration programs to compare the effectiveness of raising the maximum grant and providing better guidance in applying for aid as a means of improving access for low-income youths. To the extent that there has been any lack of response to labor market changes, it has been among low-income families. Moreover, given the ambiguous evidence on the impact of Pell grants on college enrollment, dollars spent on simplifying the process of applying for aid may have larger effects on college enrollment than equivalent spending on raising the Pell grant maximum.

Second, in the meantime it would be worth shifting Pell grant spending toward students more likely to be on the margin of college entry. Pell grant spending, for instance, could be front-loaded to students who are in their first two years of undergraduate training. Since 1980, the real value of the maximum Pell grant—a convenient measure of the aid available to the neediest students—has fallen by 35 percent while the average tuition at a public two-year and four-year university has risen by more than 80 percent. Slightly over one-quarter of Pell grant spending is devoted to students in their third and fourth years of college. (The proportion going to students in their first two years is far more than half since Pell grant recipients often complete less than two years of college.) Limiting eligibility to those in their first two years of college would allow for an increase in the maximum grant for such students.

Third, the formula for calculating a family's expected contribution should be retargeted toward low-income families. The progressivity of the formula has been eroded over time, as housing assets have been excluded and those with more than one child in college receive even larger discounts. Under the pre-1998 formula, a youth from a family of four with one parent working and no income or savings of his own qualified for the maximum Pell grant of $2,640 if the family's income was below $24,000. Pell grant eligibility then phased out for such a family at an income just below $40,000. When the Pell grant maximum was raised to $3,000, families with incomes above $40,000 became eligible. Without a change in the expected family contribution schedule, raising the Pell grant maximum has become a costly way to provide support to low-income families since it opens up eligibility for many middle-income families as well. Increasing the benefit reduction rate on family income lowers the cost of providing aid to the neediest students.

The combination of proposals—front-loading the Pell grant program and adjusting the expected family contribution schedule—would have a number of advantages. Most important, it would target a larger share of aid to those on the margin of college attendance. Presumably, a larger share of those who currently remain in college for their third or fourth year would have attended college anyway.

Any increase in the Pell grant maximum, however, raises concerns of abuse, particularly by for-profit schools. Although fears of student aid abuse have subsided somewhat in the past few years as the institutions with the highest student loan default rates have been denied eligibility for federal student aid programs, any increase in the Pell grant maximum increases the temptation for abuse and thus raises the potential for scandal. (As mentioned, because it is a 100 percent credit for the first $1,000 in expenditures, the Hope tax credit will provide similar opportunities for abuse.) Although any increase in Pell grant spending must be accompanied by redoubled efforts to ensure that students have adequate information about program quality (graduation rates, placement rates, etc.) and that the process of program accreditation at the state level is rigorous, some abuse is an unavoidable byproduct of providing this grant aid.

Fourth, income-contingent loan forgiveness should be expanded as an alternative form of means testing. Most of our current financial aid programs are provided on a backward-looking basis. Eligibility for Pell grants and subsidized federal loans, for instance, is based on a family's and youth's income and assets in the prior year. In contrast, the income-contingent loan option (created during the 1992 reauthorization) makes a forward-looking evaluation of a person's means—forgiving remaining balances for those with low incomes for twenty-five years after college. Though the repayment schedule in the current program has been designed primarily to lengthen the duration of repayment rather than to forgive many loans, the program could easily be adapted to be more generous, for instance, by lowering the percentage of the adjusted gross income that a person is expected to devote to loan repayment.

As an alternative to the traditional form of means testing in student aid, forward-looking means testing has several advantages. First, it offers "insurance" to both high- and low-income families concerned about whether their children will be able to shoulder their student debt. Under the current system of backward-looking means testing, students from low-income households who prosper after college are treated equivalently to similar students who struggle in the labor market. Moreover, middle- and higher-income youths who have difficulties after high school are offered little relief short of defaulting on student loans. Although the average return to education may have increased, the variance in earnings within each educational group has also increased; by implication, then, the variance in returns to education has risen. Diverting some subsidies currently distributed according to a backward-looking assessment of a youth's resources would provide more insurance in the face of the rising risk.

Second, forward-looking means testing does not involve the same difficulty in distinguishing dependent students—whose parents' resources are considered in the determination of need—from independent students. The distinction between dependent and independent students becomes moot if subsidies are dispersed on the basis of future incomes rather than on a single year of income and assets.

Third, the most onerous administrative burden imposed by our financial aid system—that parents and students spend long hours each year filing complicated financial aid forms—could be lightened if a larger share of available subsidies were provided on a forward-looking basis. Indeed, transferring other loan subsidies—in-school interest subsidies, preferential rates on Perkins loans, etc.—into income-contingent loan forgiveness would relieve millions of parents of the need to file financial aid forms every year to establish their eligibility. If we eliminated the distinction between subsidized and unsubsidized loans, there would be little reason for many parents to file a financial aid form. Only those seeking institutional aid (primarily the quarter of students who attend private four-year institutions) or Pell grant or federal work study aid would have to file a financial aid application.

Fourth, forward-looking means testing can greatly diminish the marginal tax rates on income and savings implicit in the financial aid formula since subsidies would be based on an entire career of income rather than "taxing" a single year of parental income or repeatedly assessing a family's stock of accumulated assets.

A formidable barrier to income contingency is the opposition of private banks that finance and collect student loans. Income contingency, however, could be delivered through the tax system merely by providing taxpayers with a tax credit when their student loan payments in a given year exceed some percentage of their income. The deductibility of student loan interest, included in the package of tax expenditures, is one way to achieve income contingency, although the $1,000 deduction is not limited to those whose loan payments represent a large share of their income.

Finally, the federal government should find ways to complement, and not just substitute for, state spending. State governments continue to provide the lion's share of subsidies to higher education. One idea would be to offer states the opportunity to "buy into" the federal loan programs by reimbursing the federal government for providing more favorable interest rates or income-contingent repayment schemes to their residents. Given the mobility of the nation's population across state lines, the federal government is in the best position to operate an income-contingent repayment scheme efficiently. To buffer the effect of public tuition increases, states may be interested in helping to provide more favorable loan terms to their residents.

Conclusion

It is no coincidence that, as the labor market increasingly values educational attainment, calls to improve the education system have become ever louder. The same labor market imperatives that drive parents to complain about quality in elementary and secondary schooling are driving the concern about affordability in postsecondary education. The impending movement of the baby-boomlet cohort into college is likely to fuel the debate over the allocation of public subsidies for college over the coming decade.

In preparing for that debate, we still need answers to some basic questions:

How well does our current set of subsidies enable worthwhile investments in college? As summarized, evidence has been often conflicting. A modest investment in an experimental evaluation of alternative student aid schemes—providing more generous grants and loans or better counseling—could go a long way toward anticipating the impact of proposed policies.

What is the payoff to college for the marginal youth? A year in college is a much more costly investment of society's resources than the private price paid by students and families. Educational expenditures per student were approximately $12,000 per year at a four-year college and approximately $6,000 per year at a public two-year college (DoE 1996, 352–53, t. 339, 340). In-state tuition at public institutions typically covers only one-quarter of these expenses. As a result, youths and families are making decisions about investing society's resources without facing the full cost of that decision. Although unmeasurable social benefits such as the political benefits of a more informed citizenry are hard to tally (and presumably are the primary reason for the public subsidy in the first place), it may be worth identifying the private payoffs to college education for the students whose decisions are affected by marginal changes in tuition and financial aid policies. Studying differences in earnings and educational attainment associated with variation in state tuition policies and proximity to college would provide one way to identify such effects.

Increasingly, families and youths have responded to the shifting winds in the labor market by enrolling in college rather than entering the labor market directly after high school. Throughout the 1980s and early 1990s, demographic trends spared taxpayers from the full expense of that change in behavior, as the size of college age cohorts shrank. The demographic tide, however, is in the midst of shifting. During the recent reauthorization of the higher education act, the nation missed an opportunity to fix some structural weaknesses in the system of financing higher education, with Congress considering only a small set of incremental reforms. Rather than accept tax relief as a substitute for sound education policy, we should undertake a more fundamental course of reform.

References

Callan, Patrick, and Joni Finney. 1993. *By Design or Default?* California Higher Education Policy Center.

Cameron, Stephen V., and James J. Heckman. 1998. "The Dynamics of Educational Attainment for Blacks, Hispanics and Whites," working paper.

Campbell, Paul R. 1994. *Population Projections for States, by Age, Race and Sex: 1993 to 2020*, U.S. Bureau of the Census, Current Population Reports, P25-1111. Washington, D.C.: Government Printing Office.

Case, Karl E., and Michael S. McPherson. 1986. "Student Aid Incentives and Parental Effort: The Impact of Need-Based Aid on Savings and Labor Supply." Technical report prepared for the Washington Office of the College Board. Washington, D.C.: CB.

Clotfelter, Charles. 1996. *Buying the Best: Cost Escalation in Elite Higher Education.* Princeton: Princeton University Press.

College Board. 1996. *Trends in Student Aid: 1986 to 1996.* Washington, D.C.: CB.

Dick, Andrew W., and Aaron S. Edlin. 1996. "The Implicit Taxes from College Financial Aid." *Journal of Public Economics.*

Edlin, Aaron S. 1993. "Is College Financial Aid Equitable and Efficient?" *Journal of Economic Perspectives* 7 (spring): 143–58.

Feldstein, Martin. 1995. "College Scholarship Rules and Private Saving." *American Economic Review* 73 (June): 398–410.

Hansen, W. Lee. 1983. "Impact of Student Financial Aid on Access." In *The Crisis in Higher Education,* edited by Joseph Froomkin. New York: Academy of Political Science.

Hansen, W. Lee, and Burton Weisbrod. 1969. "The Distribution of Costs and Direct Benefits of Public Higher Education: The Case of California." *Journal of Human Resources* 4 (spring): 176–91.

Kane, Thomas J. 1994. "College Entry by Blacks since 1970: The Role of College Costs, Family Background and Returns to Education." *Journal of Political Economy* 102: 878–911.

———. 1995a. "Rising Public College Tuition and College Entry: How Well Do Public Subsidies Promote Access to College?" Working Paper 5164, National Bureau of Economic Research, Cambridge.

———. 1995b. "Postsecondary and Vocational Education: Keeping Track of the College Track." In *Indicators of Children's Well-Being:*

Conference Papers, Institute for Research on Poverty Special Report, SR 60b.

―――. 1997. "Beyond Tax Relief: Long-Term Challenges in Financing Higher Education." *National Tax Journal* 50, no. 2: 335–49.

―――. 1998. "Savings Incentives for Higher Education." *National Tax Journal* 51, no. 3: 609–20.

Leslie, Lawrence L., and Paul T. Brinkman. 1988. *The Economic Value of Higher Education.* New York: Macmillan.

Manski, Charles, and David Wise. 1983. *College Choice in America.* Cambridge: Harvard University Press.

McPherson, Michael, and Morton Owen Schapiro. 1991. *Keeping College Affordable.* Washington, D.C.: Brookings Institution.

National Commission on the Cost of Higher Education. 1998. *Straight Talk about College Costs and Prices.* Washington, D.C.: American Institutes for Research.

New Jersey Commission on Financing Postsecondary Education. 1975. *The Needs and Resources of Undergraduate Students in Postsecondary Education in the State of New Jersey.* Princeton: NJCFPE.

Orfield, Gary. 1992. "Money, Equity and College Access." *Harvard Educational Review* 72, no. 3 (fall): 337–72.

Pechman, Joseph A. 1970. "The Distributional Effects of Public Higher Education in California." *Journal of Human Resources* 5 (summer): 361–70.

U.S. Bureau of the Census. 1995. *Statistical Abstract of the United States.* Washington, D.C.: Government Printing Office.

U.S. Department of Education, National Center for Education Statistics. 1996. *Digest of Education Statistics 1996.* NCES 96–133. Washington, D.C.: Government Printing Office.

5

Can Tuition Policy Combat Rising Wage Inequality?

Stephen V. Cameron and James J. Heckman

The recent rise in the economic return to higher education and the decline in the real wages of male high school graduates have stimulated interest in policies that promote skill formation in order to reduce wage inequality. The increase in the college wage premium began in the late 1970s and is especially pronounced among the most recent work force entrants. It is a major contributor to the recent rise in wage inequality.

As often happens in popular discussions of policy problems, a fifteen-year trend of rising wage inequality is now widely assumed to be an immutable feature of the modern economy. This view is held despite a growing body of empirical evidence that the trend toward rising wage inequality has now abated (Krueger 1997). A recent analysis of wage inequality in the American economy demonstrates that without any intervention beyond the large subsidies already in place, the induced increase in the supply of skills to the economy will restore the variance of log wages to its pre-1979 level (Heckman, Lochner, and Taber 1998a). The problem of rising wage inequality in the past fifteen years is localized in the experience of cohorts of low-skill workers in the labor market around the onset of skill-biased technical change. In the long run, workers of all ability levels benefit from technological change. If any policy intervention is warranted, it should be in the form of wage subsidies and income supplements directed toward specific cohorts of low-skill workers caught up in the transition to a new high-

Portions of this chapter were first presented in Heckman's Gilbert Lecture at Rochester, April 1996. This research was supported by NSF 93-21-048, a grant from the Mellon Foundation, and NIH grants 5R01HD32058-03 and 1R01HD34958-01. Early drafts of this work appeared in 1990 and 1992. We thank Marvin Kosters for helpful comments.

skill economy and not in the form of policies to augment the current large subsidies that promote skill formation.

Despite this evidence, many analysts concerned about rising wage inequality have advocated increases in the already substantial public subsidies to promote enrollment in college. The most popular argument in support of enhanced subsidies is that when more people obtain a college education, a wider group in society benefits from rising skill prices (Reich 1991). An economically more sophisticated version of the argument notes that when a greater proportion of the work force is educated, the high school graduates who choose to remain uneducated become more scarce. This reduction in their relative numbers increases the price of their skill and thus helps to alleviate their plight and to reduce wage inequality (Heckman 1996).

A third argument is intergenerational in character and assumes a particular form of market failure. It is based on a strongly positive empirical relationship between family income and college enrollment. It starts by noting that enrollment in college has been concentrated among persons from higher-income families (figure 5–1). The children of high-income parents responded most to the rise in skill differentials that started in the late 1970s. This response threatens to perpetuate inequality across generations by creating a more stratified society. Many attribute this relationship to short-term credit constraints experienced by families in the years their children are making college enrollment decisions as well as rising tuition costs and suggest that policies should be structured to eliminate a source of bias against the poor that appears to be an important feature of the American educational system. Since minorities are overrepresented in the lower quartiles of the income distribution, tuition and family income policy are advocated to prevent a further widening of the educational gap between majority white and minority groups evident in figure 5–2 and to promote racial and ethnic equality.

This chapter evaluates these arguments and the empirical evidence that supports them. The first two arguments ignore the substantial cost of changing the level of education in society at large to alleviate the problem of rising wage inequality. They further ignore the self-correcting features of the American economy. As relative supplies of skilled labor continue to increase in response to the rising return to skill, inequality is likely to decrease. The third argument has superficial plausibility and is often invoked to justify further subsidies to higher education (see, for example, chapter 4 in this volume). It interprets the empirical correlation between family income and college enrollment in only one of many possible ways.

FIGURE 5–1
COLLEGE PARTICIPATION BY EIGHTEEN- TO TWENTY-FOUR-YEAR-OLD
HIGH SCHOOL GRADUATES AND GED HOLDERS, 1970–1993
(percent)

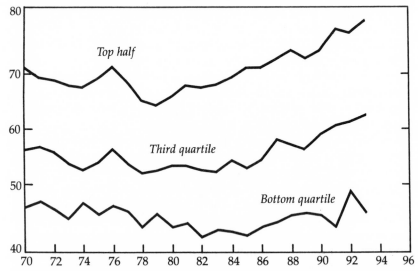

SOURCE: These numbers were computed from 1971–1989 CPS P-20 School Reports and the 1990–1993 October CPS data files.

At a strictly descriptive level, a family income–schooling relationship can arise from short-run credit constraints or long-run family and environmental factors that make some persons better suited to participate in education than others. The weight of the evidence presented in this chapter suggests that family income, as measured by the surveys used to estimate the relationship demonstrated in figure 5–1, is better viewed as a determinant of long-term factors that shape the ability and motivation of children. We offer evidence that quick-fix income or tuition supplements like Hope tax credits or Pell grant money offered to potential college students late in their teenage years are unlikely to do much to ameliorate the observed pattern of schooling enrollment by family income.

Interventions at earlier stages of the life cycle are more likely to be effective in alleviating ethnic and racial schooling gaps. Skill formation is a lifetime affair. A student must finish high school before being able to graduate from college. Much of the gap between minority and majority college enrollment levels can be attributed to gaps in high school attainment and in achievement at earlier stages of the life cycle.

FIGURE 5–2
COLLEGE-ENTRY PROPORTIONS OF TWENTY-ONE- TO TWENTY-FOUR-YEAR-OLD HIGH SCHOOL GRADUATES AND GED HOLDERS, 1970–1996
(percent)

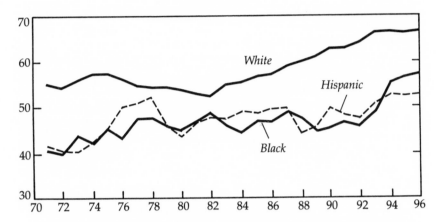

NOTE: Racial-ethnic groups are defined mutually exclusively.
SOURCE: The numbers represent three-year moving averages of March CPS data (two-year averages for 1971 and 1996).

Magnitudes of Subsidies to Reverse Rising Wage Inequality

One approach to evaluating the potential effects of educational subsidies on reducing wage inequality starts with a demand equation relating the changes over time in the relative wages of skilled and unskilled workers to relative quantities of the two factors: (% change over time in skilled wages relative to unskilled wages) = (trend) − b (% change over time in quantities of skilled labor relative to unskilled labor).[1] The thrust of this equation is that the greater the growth in the ratio of skilled to unskilled workers, the slower the growth in the wages of skilled

---

1. In symbols, where W_s is the wage of skilled labor, W_u is the wage of unskilled labor, Q_s is the quantity of skilled labor, and Q_u is the quantity of unskilled labor,

$$\Delta \ln \left[\frac{W_s(t)}{W_u(t)} \right] = \alpha - \frac{1}{\sigma} \Delta \ln \left[\frac{Q_s(t)}{Q_u(t)} \right]$$

where Δ denotes change and ln denotes logarithm. In this equation, α is the trend rate of relative wage growth, and σ, a positive number, is the elasticity of substitution between the two types of labor. The higher σ, the more substitutable are skilled workers for unskilled workers, $b = 1/\sigma$.

workers compared with those of unskilled workers. The greater the trend, the more the technology is shifting in favor of skilled labor over time and the more likely it is that wage differentials between skilled and unskilled workers will increase over time. Katz and Murphy (1992) estimate this equation for the United States over the period 1963–1987.[2]

With that definition of college and high school skill groups, the 1979–1989 percentage change in relative wages is roughly fourteen percentage points. To reverse the ten-year trend by increasing the relative supply of skilled workers requires a once-and-for-all increase of approximately 20 percent in the number of high-skill persons in the work force. With the definitions of skill groups employed by Katz and Murphy, college equivalents are 40 percent of the work force, and high school equivalents are 60 percent. For a 1990 work force of 120 million, about 5.4 million people need to be transformed to college equivalents to reverse the decade-long erosion of real wages.[3] To maintain this gain in relative wages against the secular trend operating against unskilled labor, about 1 million additional skilled persons need to be added to the work force each year on top of the once-and-for-all change of 5.4 million.[4]

As a benchmark, the annual supply of high-skill equivalents to the U.S. economy in the early 1990s is approximately 1.8 million. Maintenance of existing skill gaps alone would require that the percentage of persons acquiring postsecondary skills would have to rise by 55 percent.[5] To phase in the additional 5.4 million people who are required to restore wage parities to their 1979 levels over ten years would require a total annual expansion of the supply of high-skill persons of 70–80 percent, depending on alternative assumptions about the retirement of unskilled older workers. To engineer such an increase through a tuition policy requires a substantial tuition reduction. With a college attendance tuition elasticity of $-.30$, which is the order of magnitude reported in the literature, the required reduction in tuition is 181

---

2. They estimate $\sigma = 1/b$ to be 1.41 with a standard error of .150, although they also suggest that a range of estimates with σ as low as .5 is also consistent with the data. Katz and Murphy estimate the trend, α, as .033 (standard error .007). Johnson (1970) reports an estimate of $\sigma = 1.50$ for the elasticity of substitution between college and high school labor. Using different measures of college and high school skill, Heckman, Lochner, and Taber (1998a, b) estimate that $\sigma = 1.44$ and $\alpha = .032$.

3. Even with their lower range estimate of $1/b = \sigma = .5$, 2 million persons need to be shifted from the unskilled to the skilled category to offset the decade-long trend against unskilled labor.

4. 400,000 for the lower-bound case.

5. 22 percent in the lower-bound case.

percent.[6] College tuition would have to be zero, and people would have to be paid to attend school. These large numbers are based on the behavioral assumption widely used in the literature (see, for example, Kane 1994 or in this volume) that prospective students act as if skill prices will not change when national tuition policies change and induce substantial numbers of people to enter college.

A more convincing evaluation of the effectiveness of a national tuition policy allows for skill prices to adjust and for agents to anticipate the adjustment and to respond appropriately. It also accounts for the tax costs of the policy and behavioral responses to the increase in taxes. We discuss such simulations below.

We proceed by first examining the conventional argument in favor of tuition subsidies: we ignore the tax consequences of raising the revenue to support the tuition supplements and ignore how rational agents who anticipate the effect of the tuition policy on skill prices respond in their schooling behavior. When these additional factors are incorporated into the analysis, the estimated effects of tuition subsidies on reducing wage inequality are substantially diminished and make tuition policy an unlikely vehicle for eliminating wage inequality. Even ignoring these factors, however, the case for expanding tuition subsidies is not strong.

The Relationship between Tuition, Family Income, and College Attendance

The empirical association between family income and college enrollment presented in figure 5–1 has attracted an enormous amount of attention in academic and policy circles. The most common interpretation of this evidence is that short-term family credit constraints prevent children from low-income families from attending school. The Pell grant program, the Hope credit program, and many other governmental educational programs are premised on this interpretation of the evidence. It is the most popular explanation for the time series of the ethnic and racial gaps in college enrollment, displayed in figure 5–2. Since minority families are concentrated in the lower quartiles of the

---

6. McPherson and Schapiro (1991) report an estimated average elasticity (with respect to net tuition) of $-.30$ ranging from $-.14$ for high school (family income $> \$30{,}000$ per year in 1978 dollars) to $-.47$ for low income (family income $\leq \$10{,}000$ per year). St. John (1993) reports $-.28$ for gross tuition. We estimate a gross tuition elasticity of $-.31$ to $-.33$ for two- and four-year schools, respectively. See Cameron and Heckman (1998b). The lower-bound case is 75 percent. These calculations were first presented in Heckman (1996).

family income distribution, their failure to respond to the increase in the economic returns to schooling is widely viewed as a manifestation of the more general phenomenon of a family income–dependent response to the rising return to skill that is evident in figure 5–1.

The common interpretation of that figure notes that real tuition costs have increased in percentage terms over the past sixteen years. At the same time, family incomes have declined among the bottom quartiles of the family income distribution. The real wages and employment of unskilled males have declined since the late 1970s. More families at the bottom of the family income distribution are headed by females with dependent children. Such families have lower earnings and income levels than families headed by males.

According to this interpretation, the dual impact of rising tuition costs and declining family resources has had a devastating impact on the college attendance decisions of children from low-income families. Based on this interpretation, policies that further subsidize the already substantial subsidies available to educate children from low-income families have been advocated, most notably by Hauser (1991, 1993) and Mortenson (1988).

Certainly, real tuition costs have risen over the past sixteen years. Between 1980 and 1997, average public posted "sticker price" tuition levels rose by 100 percent at public four-year colleges and universities and by 77 percent at public two-year colleges (NCES 1997). At the same time, government subsidies to higher education are already large. For public institutions, nearly half of all expenditures are covered by direct appropriations from state and local governments. Revenue generated by public institutions in 1994 was approximately $87 billion.[7] Tuition and fees accounted for only 25 percent of revenues; direct grants, appropriations, and contracts from local, state, and federal governments to these institutions made up another 66 percent; and the remaining 9 percent came from endowment revenue and gifts.[8] In addition, the federal government spent another $6 billion on direct grants to low-income students and another $7 billion on subsidies to student loan programs.[9] These funds serve to offset some of the remaining 25 per-

---

7. On average, revenue and expenditures were about equal. This figure excludes revenue from and expenditures on hospitals and other auxiliary enterprises (NCES 1997).

8. Because college training is produced jointly with research in some cases, the size of the subsidy to higher education may be slightly overstated; because the figures we state are for public and not private institutions, however, the figure understates total governmental support to higher education.

9. Total loan disbursements were about $22 billion, of which approximately one-third was a subsidy.

cent of total cost of college borne by students. About half this subsidy goes to students in public institutions (NCES 1997). All told, individuals attending public institutions of higher education pay on average less than 20 percent of the total direct cost of attending college. (Direct cost does not include forgone earnings.) Moreover, a substantial fraction of the 20 percent of the total costs borne by individuals is actually paid by private foundations and charities that extend aid directly to students.

Popular discussions of education policy often confuse the question of whether education should be subsidized with the question of whether the already substantial public subsidies to higher education should be increased. The conventional wisdom is that credit constraints are binding for prospective college students from low-income families and have become more stringent as the poor families have become poorer at precisely the same time that tuition costs have risen along with the rise in the return to education.[10] The argument is made that since government policy has contributed to the rising inequity in schooling among different family income groups through expansion of tuition costs, policy can also help to eliminate it. We now present reasons to doubt the received wisdom.

The Positive Relationship between Family Income and College Enrollment

The argument that family credit constraints are the most plausible explanation for figure 5–1 starts by noting that human capital is different from physical capital. With the abolition of slavery and indentured servitude, there is no asset market for human capital. People cannot sell rights to their future labor earnings to lenders to secure financing for their human capital investments. Even if they could, there would be substantial problems in enforcing performance of contracts on future earnings, given that persons control their own labor supply and the effort and quality of their work. The lack of collateral and the inability to monitor effort are widely cited reasons for current large-scale government interventions to finance education.

If people had to rely on their own resources to finance all their schooling costs, no doubt the level of educational attainment in American society would decline. To the extent that subsidies do not cover the full costs of tuition, persons are forced to pay tuition through private

---

10. The rise in tuition costs is linked, in part, to the rise in the economic return to college education since college-educated labor is a major input into the educational system.

loans, through work while in college, or through forgone consumption. Children from families with higher income have access to resources that children from families with lower income do not have, although children from higher-income families still depend on the good will of their parents to gain access to funds. Limited access to credit markets means that the costs of funds are higher for the children of the poor, and this limits their enrollment in college.

Current tax law exacerbates these problems. Borrowing costs for education cannot be written off against taxes. Even if they could be itemized, few poor families find it profitable to itemize deductions. Until recently, the only exception to the nondeductibility of interest in the current tax law was mortgage interest. Under the new law, deductions for student loans are available. These deductions benefit persons who itemize and are unlikely to have much effect on college attendance for poor children. All families can itemize mortgage interest payments in declaring their taxes. Poorer families, however, are much less likely to own their own homes, and hence fewer of them are eligible to use mortgages on their homes to finance the schooling of their children.

The purchase of education may also be governed by the same principles that govern the purchase of other goods. There is, undoubtedly, a consumption component to education.[11] Families with higher incomes buy more education for their children and buy higher-quality education as well. This factor partly explains the levels of the relationships presented in figure 5–1.

An alternative and not necessarily mutually exclusive interpretation of the evidence is that long-run family and environmental factors play a decisive role in shaping the ability and expectations of children. Families with higher levels of resources produce higher-quality children who are better able to perform in school and take advantage of the new market for skills.

Children whose parents have higher incomes have access to better-quality secondary schools. Children's tastes for education and their expectations about their life chances are shaped by those of their parents. Educated parents are better able to develop the scholastic aptitude in their children by assisting and directing their studies. The influences of family factors that are present from birth through high school completion accumulate over many years to produce ability and college readiness. High school certification is required for college attendance. While there is a racial and ethnic gap in college enrollment among high school graduates, there is also a substantial racial and ethnic gap in high school graduation (figure 5–3). There is already a substantial gap in

---

11. Lazear (1977) presents some evidence on this question.

FIGURE 5–3
DISTRIBUTION OF SCHOOLING ATTAINMENT

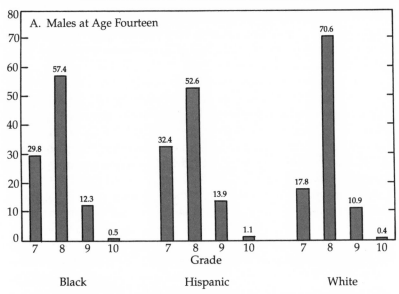

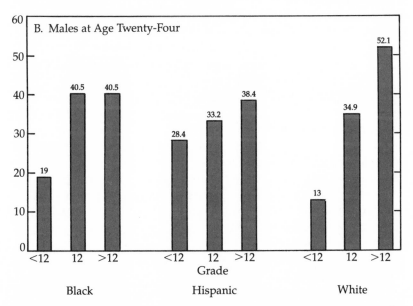

NOTE: Years of schooling are shown at the base. Category <12 represents less than a high school diploma, and category >12 represents college attendance.
SOURCE: National Longitudinal Survey of Youth, 1979–1989.

schooling completion by age fourteen. A large part of the racial and ethnic gap in college attendance can be explained by the gap in high school certification. High school certification depends on completing the eleventh grade, completing the tenth grade is required to attend the eleventh, and so forth. Families play an important role in shaping the performance of children at each stage of the educational process.

In addition, a feedback process may operate. Children who grow up in inferior environments may expect less of themselves and may not fully develop their academic potential because they see little hope for ever being able to complete college or use their schooling in any effective way. There is also the element of uncertainty. People from disadvantaged environments where no one has previously gone to college will face greater uncertainty about their prospects for success and the steps needed to achieve it.

This alternative interpretation, which stresses the role of family and the environment, does not necessarily rule out the importance of short-term borrowing constraints as a partial explanation for figures 5–1 and 5–2. If the finances of poor but motivated families hinder them from providing decent elementary and secondary schooling for their children, however, and produce a low level of college readiness, government policy aimed at reducing the short-term borrowing constraints for the college expenses of those children is unlikely to be effective. Policy that improves the environments that shape ability may be a more effective avenue for increasing college enrollment in the long run. The issue could be settled empirically, although surprisingly little data have been brought to bear on it.

The distinction between long-run family factors that promote college readiness and short-term borrowing constraints can be conceptualized by imagining an experiment in which a random sample of families is drawn and some of the families win a million dollar lottery at different points in the life cycle of their children. Those who win as their children near high school completion have little opportunity to make cumulative long-run family investments that contribute to college-preparedness. There would be little effect of the newly acquired wealth on the college attendance of their children if college readiness and ability are the decisive elements in producing enrollment in college.

For lottery winners with young children, a much larger response to the lottery would be expected in terms of the college attendance of their children if parents invest in better schools and more academic opportunities for their children over a longer horizon. If short-term credit market constraints are the significant factor governing college attendance, then we expect a large response in college enrollments by children of previously poor families regardless of the age of their children at the time the lottery was won.

If public policy aims to encourage college attendance, a focus on improving the environments of children and improving preparation for college may be more effective than grant or loan programs to economically or cognitively disadvantaged children in their late teenage years. If ability promotes academic progress, then early interventions lead to higher achievement. What is known about ability is that it is formed relatively early in life and becomes less malleable as children age. By age fourteen, basic abilities seem to be fairly well set (see the evidence summarized in Heckman 1995). By the time individuals finish high school and scholastic ability is determined, the scope of public policy for promoting college attendance is greatly diminished.

Only to the extent that the family income of able high school graduates falls below levels required to pay for college will short-term credit market constraints hinder college entry. Given the current college financial support arrangements that are available to low-income and minority children, we now demonstrate that the phenomenon of bright students being denied access to college because of credit constraints is empirically unimportant.

Tuition Costs and College Attendance

Thus far we have focused solely on the role of family income in explaining participation in college. With or without credit market constraints, a rise in tuition will reduce college attendance because it reduces the net returns (labor market payoffs less costs) to college. Moreover, if consumption benefits are important in explaining the demand for a college education, a rise in tuition acts like a rise in the price of any good: higher prices lead to lower demand. Evidence of an enrollment response to tuition changes is not informative about the empirical importance of borrowing constraints.

It is easy to exaggerate the contribution of tuition costs toward explaining the gap in the college attendance of children from rich and poor families. Substantial loan and aid programs already are targeted toward students from poorer families. At public two- and four-year institutions in the United States in 1996, average costs of tuition and fees were about $2,300.[12] For community colleges, where 40 per-

---

12. These figures are for in-state tuition. The proper concept of cost is based on the marginal room and board cost that arises from attending college, not the total cost, since people have to eat or sleep whether or not they go to college. Unfortunately, we do not know this marginal cost and assume that it is zero.

cent of college students are found, tuitions are even lower. To offset these costs, both the Pell grant and subsidized student loan programs are available to children of low-income families.[13] Eligibility is determined by actual college costs and an estimated parental contribution that depends on travel expenses and allowances for miscellaneous expenses, the student's dependency status, family income and assets, and the number of other children in a family in college or postsecondary vocational training programs. In 1997, a first-year dependent college student was eligible for a maximum of about $8,000 in federal grants and subsidized loans. No minimum contribution toward estimated college costs was required from the student or the parents.[14] In round figures, the $8,000 maximum benefit consisted of $2,500 in Pell grants, $2,500 in Stafford loans, and $3,000 in Perkins loans. The maximum rose to $11,000 for third- and fourth-year college students as subsidized loan limits rise. If a student lived at home, room and board charges were subtracted from the estimated cost figure, but transportation costs were added to determine total aid eligibility.

A host of other federal programs directs money to students in some form or another. These include guaranteed but otherwise unsubsidized Plus loans to parents, campus work-study, Veterans Administration aid, aid to present and past military personnel, and aid from employers who receive federal tax write-offs for underwriting employee college costs. In addition, eligible students have access to many other state and institutional subsidies. In 1996, total institutional subsidies alone approximated the size of the entire Pell grant program (College Board 1997).

Discussions of college tuition policy focus too often on the elite public and private institutions and ignore the broad spectrum of community colleges and public four-year colleges that are available to students. They often overlook the rapid growth of community colleges in the past twenty-five years. More than 40 percent of all current college students are in community colleges. These colleges offer low tuitions (typically about $1,300 per year in 1997 dollars) and flexible schedules that allow students to work and attend college. There are many more community colleges (1,036) than four-year colleges (604), and most prospective students have one nearby so access to them is not a serious problem. Costs of room and board can be avoided by living with par-

---

13. Stafford and Perkins loans are the principal components of the loan package.

14. Before 1993, students or their families were required to make a minimum contribution of around $800 toward college costs before student aid became available. In 1993, the minimum requirement was eliminated.

ents.[15] Evidence reported by Kane and Rouse (1995) suggests that the economic return to a year at a community college is the same as the economic return at a four-year college. Taken at face value, their evidence suggests that there is no compromise in generating human capital by attending a community college for the first two years of the college experience.

The growth in community colleges is an institutional response to the rigid schedules, high tuition costs, and lack of access characteristic of four-year schools. Many current arguments about the costs of attending college were more valid twenty-five years ago than they are now. In the current environment, with the community college institution in place and with generous loan and grant programs available, the arguments that tuition costs and commuting are major barriers to college attendance by the poor are implausible.

To strengthen this argument, we note that the take-up rate on Pell grants and Perkins loans is low (Orfield 1992). Many more funds are available to potential low-income students than are spent. Binding credit constraints are not a plausible explanation for the underutilization of these resources. It is more likely that many eligible persons perceive that even with a substantial tuition subsidy, the returns to college education for them are too low to pay for the forgone earnings required to attend school.

The Unimportance of Short-Term Credit Constraints

Empirical work on estimating the effects of family income and tuition costs on college attendance has been hindered by a lack of data. Few data sets are available with information on college attendance and parental income. Fewer still have information on college attendance and family income and family wealth. Even fewer follow families over time to enable analysts to examine how unanticipated changes in family income, of the sort envisioned in the hypothetical lottery experiment discussed earlier, change the schooling of children.

Data on unanticipated changes in income would be especially valuable. If families are truly constrained by credit, unanticipated increases and decreases in family income of the same magnitude would affect schooling attainment in an asymmetric fashion. If persons are already not attending college by virtue of being credit constrained, reducing their income further has no effect on their college attendance. Raising their income may increase their schooling. This asymmetry in

---

15. Callan (1997) presents a useful overview of the American community college system.

the response to positive and negative income innovations is the signature of a credit-constrained position both for education and other investment decisions.

Elsewhere (Cameron and Heckman 1998b), we use the National Longitudinal Survey of Youth (NLSY) data that provide information on ability, family income, and schooling to shed light on the importance and interpretation to be placed on the family income–schooling relationship.[16] We summarize the main findings from a companion paper.[17] A major limitation of these data is that family income is measured at only a few time points. This limitation precludes us from estimating the responses of child education decisions to anticipated and unanticipated changes in family income to operationalize the earlier thought experiment or to test the asymmetry in schooling responses to positive and negative income innovations.[18]

Panel A of figure 5–3 shows the distribution of male schooling attainment at ages fourteen by race and ethnic groups and panel B shows the comparison distribution at age twenty-four. There are large disparities between racial-ethnic groups. The two most important features of panel B are the large differences in college attendance (category >12 on the figure) and high school dropping out (<12).[19] Whites are about 12–14 percent more likely to enroll in college by age twenty-

16. The widely used Current Population Survey data have problems that limit their usefulness in estimating the determinants of college participation. See the discussion in Appendix A.

17. The NLSY is a panel data set, with information on family income and schooling, that annually surveys more than 12,000 young men and women in the United States starting in 1979. Continuous schooling histories are available from January 1978. We use only male samples because their schooling decisions are less complicated by fertility considerations. In addition, to have complete schooling histories beginning at age fifteen as well as test score information on individuals before they completed high school, we restrict our study to young men age sixteen or less in January 1978. Our sample is based on the 1979–1989 waves of the National Longitudinal Survey of Youth (the military subsample and the non-black, non-Hispanic disadvantaged samples are excluded). More details of the data can be found in Cameron and Heckman (1998b).

18. Even if we had a good time series of family income, there is a nontrivial problem in decomposing it into components that are anticipated and those that are not. Statistical decompositions of time series data into predictable and unpredictable components do not necessarily estimate the predictable components as perceived, and acted on, by households. See, for example, the discussion in Browning, Hansen, and Heckman (1999).

19. To accord with census conventions, GED attainment and traditional high school graduation have been combined into the category 12. Minorities take GEDs at roughly twice the rate of whites. See Cameron and Heckman (1993).

four, and Hispanics are about 17 percent more likely to have not completed high school. Analyses for later ages confirm that there is little college entry or high school completion after age twenty-four.

Panel A of the figure shows important early differences in the distributions of completed schooling. At age fourteen, the modal grade is eight. While all racial-ethnic groups are about equally likely to be above grade eight, minorities are 12–15 percent more likely to be below the modal grade. Furthermore, individuals at grade levels below the modal grade are much more likely to drop out of high school and more likely not to enter college if they actually go on to complete high school. Later high school graduation and college entry chances are highly correlated with early schooling attainment by age.

Despite these early disparities, most of the difference in final schooling attainment emerges after age sixteen.[20] Most high school certification follows the traditional pattern and occurs by age nineteen. Most first-time college entry, too, follows immediately after high school completion. High school completion rates are higher for whites at age twenty-four than for minorities (87 percent compared with 81 percent for blacks and 72 percent for Hispanics) and certification of a general equivalency diploma is much higher for minorities. Approximately 11 percent of whites earn high school credentials through the GED program compared with 17 percent of blacks and 22 percent of Hispanics. For both GED completers and high school graduates, about 90 percent of college enrollment occurs within two years of high school certification.[21]

Table 5–1 presents differentials in college-entry rates. For cohorts making schooling decisions in the early 1980s, it breaks out two- and four-year college-entry patterns for persons who have completed high school by age twenty-four because two-year and four-year colleges have different costs of attendance. White graduates are more likely to enter college than are blacks (by seven percentage points) or Hispanic graduates (by three percentage points). White GED recipients are more likely to attend college. Whites have the highest four-year college-entry rate and Hispanics the lowest. Hispanics, however, show the highest two-year entry rate, which is partly attributable to the regional concentration of Hispanics in states such as California and Texas with extensive community college networks and low tuition costs during the period of our study.

---

20. This finding is due in part to compulsory schooling attendance laws and to the lack of labor market opportunities for people younger than sixteen.

21. Patterns of dropping out and college delay are explored in detail by Cameron and Heckman (1998b).

TABLE 5–1
COLLEGE ENTRY BY TYPE OF COLLEGE FIRST ATTENDED FOR HIGH
SCHOOL GRADUATES AND GED RECIPIENTS AT AGE TWENTY-FOUR

Group	Four-year	Two-year	Never attended
High school graduates			
Whites	.38	.25	.37
	(.01)	(.01)	(.01)
Blacks	.33	.23	.44
	(.02)	(.02)	(.02)
Hispanics	.29	.31	.40
	(.03)	(.03)	(.03)
GED recipients			
Whites	.12	.22	.66
	(.03)	(.03)	(.03)
Blacks	.08	.15	.77
	(.02)	(.04)	(.03)
Hispanics	.10	.17	.73
	(.03)	(.03)	(.03)

NOTE: Standard errors of the means are in parentheses.
SOURCE: NLSY data (1979–1989); Cameron and Heckman (1998b).

Table 5–2 combines GED recipients and high school graduates and shows the same proportions broken down by the position of family income in terms of quartiles of the white family-income distribution. College attendance rates, for instance, are shown for the children of families in the top quartile of the white family-income distribution. The same income cutoffs in the white distribution are used to categorize blacks and Hispanics. As the table indicates, blacks and Hispanics are underrepresented in the top category because of their lower position in the family-income distribution.[22] As family income increases, youths of all racial and ethnic backgrounds are more likely to enter college.[23]

22. Parental family income is measured between ages thirteen and seventeen. The income distribution used to compute the categories in table 5–2 does not represent the population distribution of white family income in the United States but the population distribution for white families with children who are recent high school completers.

23. The only exception is a curious rise in noncollege attendance for whites as we go from the bottom to the third quartile. This rise, however, is not statistically significant. This fact seems to be due to the large number of white youths from the bottom quartile who attend two-year college.

TABLE 5–2
COLLEGE ENTRY BY AGE TWENTY-FOUR FOR HIGH SCHOOL
GRADUATES AND GED HOLDERS BY TYPE OF COLLEGE
FIRST ATTENDED AND QUARTILE OF THE WHITE
FAMILY-INCOME DISTRIBUTION

Group	Type of School			% of Total Group
	Four-year	Two-year	Both	
Total college entry				
Whites	.35	.26	.61	100
	(.01)	(.01)	(.01)	
Blacks	.29	.21	.50	100
	(.02)	(.02)	(.02)	
Hispanics	.25	.28	.53	100
	(.02)	(.02)	(.03)	
Top quartile or equivalent				
Whites	.50	.27	.77	25
	(.03)	(.02)	(.03)	
Blacks	.47	.30	.77	5
	(.08)	(.07)	(.07)	
Hispanics	.39	.18	.58	10
	(.08)	(.06)	(.08)	
Second quartile or equivalent				
Whites	.36	.26	.62	25
	(.03)	(.02)	(.03)	
Blacks	.43	.17	.60	9
	(.07)	(.05)	(.05)	
Hispanics	.37	.35	.72	14
	(.07)	(.07)	(.06)	
Third quartile or equivalent				
Whites	.28	.25	.53	25
	(.03)	(.03)	(.03)	
Blacks	.30	.22	.51	17
	(.04)	(.04)	(.05)	
Hispanics	.27	.28	.55	22
	(.04)	(.05)	(.05)	

(Table continues)

TABLE 5–2 (continued)

Group	Four-year	Two-year	Both	% of Total Group
	Type of School			
Fourth quartile or equivalent				
Whites	.27	.25	.52	25
	(.03)	(.03)	(.03)	
Blacks	.25	.22	.47	70
	(.02)	(.02)	(.02)	
Hispanics	.19	.30	.49	54
	(.03)	(.02)	(.03)	
Families with equal white-family income[a]				
Blacks	.36	.23	.59	100
	(.04)	(.03)	(.04)	
Hispanics	.30	.28	.58	100
	(.05)	(.04)	(.05)	

NOTE: Standard errors of the means are in parentheses.
a. The proportion of blacks and Hispanics who would attend college if their family-income distributions were equated to the white distribution with the proportions shown.
SOURCE: National Longitudinal Survey of Youth.

For all race groups, the chance of attending a four-year college rises with family income. All groups are about equally sensitive to income differences. Hispanics have the lowest rate of four-year college attendance in the top quartile and the lowest overall. The gap in four-year attendance rates for Hispanics in the top and bottom quartiles is twenty percentage points. The gap for blacks is seventeen percentage points and twenty-one percentage points for whites. Two-year attendance shows no definite pattern. Moving up the family-income scale, more children enter college, but there appears to be substitution from two-year to four-year colleges as family income increases.

An interesting counterfactual question is how the white-minority gap would differ if blacks and Hispanics had the same family-income distribution as whites. The answer to this question is given in the last two rows of the table,[24] which show the fraction of blacks and Hispanics going to college when family-income distributions are equated to the white distribution. Comparing the data with the actual total enrollment rates shows that, for blacks, nine percentage points of the eleven percentage point gap in total college entry is made up by equalizing

24. This exercise amounts to a simple averaging of the numbers in columns 1–3 of the first through fourth quartiles with the appropriate weights.

family income. For Hispanics, all but three percentage points of the college attendance gap is explained. Hence, these numbers reveal that family income is an important factor for both Hispanics and blacks in determining both college entry and type of college attended.

Table 5–3 summarizes the differences in family background, ability, labor market characteristics, location, and tuition costs among blacks, whites, and Hispanics. Some differences arise from the different geographical distributions of these groups. Family background differences favor whites. Minorities live in geographical areas with lower tuition costs and lower commuting costs. Features of local labor markets tend to be neutral across race groups. Measures of scholastic ability are largest for whites, intermediate for Hispanics, and lowest for blacks. These univariate relationships indicate that tuition costs play a small role in accounting for racial and ethnic differences and that scholastic ability plays a much more substantial role. Appendix B provides a more extensive discussion of these univariate differences. We now summarize a multivariate analysis of the data that confirms the initial impressions obtained from the univariate analyses.

A Life Cycle Analysis. In Cameron and Heckman (1998b), we extend the univariate analysis of the preceding subsection to estimate the contribution of family income, family background, scholastic ability, tuition costs, and opportunities in unskilled labor to schooling attainment by grade for white, black, and Hispanic males. College attendance is analyzed as a sequence of grade-by-grade decisions made at each age about staying in school. Our econometric procedure adjusts for the effects of differential survival of the most able and the most motivated and avoids the bias that plagues previous studies of educational attainment that do not adjust for the differential compositions of samples in terms of the distributions of the unobservables among groups across the various grade transitions (see the methodological discussion in Cameron and Heckman [1998a,b]). From our estimates, it is possible to determine where in the life cycle of schooling ethnic and racial gaps appear and what factors contribute most to creating them.

This section uses the estimates presented in our companion paper to address two questions. First, which variables have the most influence on schooling attainment? Second, is the estimated influence of family income on college attendance a consequence of long-run family effects or short-term borrowing constraints?

We answer the first question, variable by variable, by equating the distribution of the characteristics for blacks, Hispanics, and whites while holding the distribution of the other characteristics at their sample levels and measuring how high school graduation and college en-

TABLE 5–3
MEAN CHARACTERISTICS BY RACE GROUP

	Whites	Blacks	Hispanics
Number of siblings[a]	2.9	4.7	4.5
	(0.05)	(0.09)	(0.12)
Highest grade, father	12.2	9.3	7.9
	(0.08)	(0.09)	(0.17)
Highest grade, mother	11.9	10.7	7.8
	(0.06)	(0.08)	(0.16)
Family income/1,000	44.8	25.4	30.3
	(0.06)	(0.05)	(0.07)
Broken home	0.13	0.43	0.27
	(0.01)	(0.02)	(0.02)
Urban resident, age 14	0.73	0.82	0.93
	(0.01)	(0.01)	(0.01)
Southern resident, age 14	0.28	0.57	0.26
	(0.01)	(0.02)	(0.02)
County annual average wage/1,000 at age 18[b]	20.1	21.0	22.3
	(0.32)	(0.12)	(0.15)
County unemployment rate at age 18	6.3	6.0	6.9
	(0.12)	(0.12)	(0.16)
Four-year-state-college average tuition at age 18[b]	1,850	1,705	1,528
	(13.6)	(17.3)	(14.3)

Two-year-state-college average tuition at age 18[b]	888 (8.9)	798 (10.6)	580 (17.0)
Two-year-county-college average tuition at age 18[b]	833 (11.2)	780 (12.5)	572 (21.4)
Four-year-college Pell grant[b]	548 (12.1)	1,260 (27.5)	1,315 (22.8)
College proximity	0.82 (.01)	0.89 (.10)	0.92 (.01)
AFQT score	71.8 (.62)	46.4 (1.1)	54.4 (1.9)

NOTE: Definitions of variables used in the schooling-transition analysis follow. Number of living siblings. Family income: A two-year average of total family income measured between ages 14 and 18. Includes all components of income including public assistance, gift income in 1994 dollars. Highest grade, father: Highest grade completed in years by father when respondent was 14. Highest grade, mother: Highest grade completed in years by mother when respondent was 14. Broken home: Absence of one or both parents from the respondent's household at age 14. South, age 14: Whether the respondent lived in the southern census region at age 14. Urban, age 14: Whether the respondent lived in an urban area at age 14. County average annual earnings: The average annual earnings per job in the county of residence as measured by earnings in low-skill industries (retail and wholesale trade, services, and so forth). Measured annually at all ages. County unemployment rate: Annual unemployment rate in county of residence. Measured annually at all ages. College tuition: Two-year or four-year public college tuition for in-state students in the individual's county (if available) or state of residence in 1994 dollars. Measured annually at all ages. Pell grant award: Imputed amount of Pell grant award for both two- and four-year public institutions in the county or state in 1994 dollars. AFQT score: Score on the Armed Forces Qualification Test. Adjusted for age at time-of-test. College proximity: Whether any public two- or four-year school operates in the county of residence. Measured at all ages and broken out by two- or four-year type. Standard errors of the means are in parentheses.

a. The large number of siblings is a consequence of size-biased sampling in the NLSY.

b. Reported in 1994 dollars. Tuition figures are for in-state students at public institutions.

SOURCE: NLSY, 1979–1989.

rollment respond.[25] We address the second question by comparing the estimated effects of family background and family resources on schooling when scholastic ability (the Armed Forces Qualification Test) is included as an explanatory variable and when it is not. We interpret AFQT as the outcome of long-term family and environmental factors produced in part from the long-term permanent income of families. To the extent that the influence of family income measured at a point in time is diminished by the inclusion of AFQT, we can conclude that long-run family factors crystallized in AFQT scores are the driving force behind schooling attainment, and not short-term credit constraints.

Previous analysts have mostly concentrated on the determinants of highest grade completed or college attendance among high school graduates. Our research recognizes that schooling attainment at any age is the outcome of previous schooling choices. The probability that a person enters college depends on high school graduation, which in turn depends on finishing grade eleven and so forth, back to the earliest schooling decisions. Researchers who have studied how family factors affect the highest grade of schooling completed cannot distinguish the influence of family income on the high school attendance decision from its effect on college entry. Family factors and other influences may affect schooling decisions differentially by age and grade level.

To sort out the influence of family income on college entry from its accumulated long-term influence, conventional methods in the educational attainment literature used by Hauser and Kane are inadequate. Our methodology enables us to separate out age-by-age influences in a general way. By analyzing the entire set of age-specific schooling decisions from age fifteen through age twenty-four, we are able to parcel out by age the influences of family income and other variables. Using our estimated econometric model, we can then evaluate the consequences of policies that seek to promote college attendance through raising high school graduation. We summarize our

25. Table 5–2 addressed a counterfactual question of this sort by looking at differences in college attendance across income quartiles. The same method can, in principle, be used more generally. It becomes unwieldy, however, in samples of the size at our disposal, and we use an econometric model based on the estimates reported in Cameron and Heckman (1998b). We use that parametric model to isolate behavioral responses to variables, and we equate the distribution of characteristics by equating means of the distribution, assuming that the variances and covariances of the regressors remain unchanged. Explorations with alternative equating schemes produce similar estimates. For the sake of brevity, we report simulations from the simplest procedures. We elaborate on this procedure below.

evidence and refer the interested reader to our papers for methodological details.[26]

Effects of Family Income, Family Background, and Other Variables. Table 5–4 presents evidence on the two questions posed in the preceding section. It analyzes the sources of schooling differences between whites and minorities by decomposing the gap in educational attainment at different stages of the life cycle into the contributions of the main explanatory variables. It also presents evidence on the robustness of family income and other family factors when AFQT is included as an explanatory variable. Because racial and ethnic groups may vary in their sensitivity to differences in family income or tuition policies, the predictions of schooling attainment displayed in the table are based on estimates of the econometric model that are made separately for each racial-ethnic group.

Panel A of table 5–4 presents counterfactual simulation results for completing ninth grade by age fifteen, the initial condition (or first schooling attainment state) for our model. Panel B presents counterfactual simulation results for completing high school (by graduation or exam certification). Panel C presents counterfactual simulation results for entry into college conditional on completing high school. Panel D presents counterfactual simulation results for entering college *not* conditioning on high school attainment. This final simulation measures the net effects of background on college entry operating through schooling completion at all prior stages and is the central focus of this chapter. The last row in each panel shows the actual white-minority gap in attainment at the stage being analyzed. In all cases, it is close to the gap predicted from the model.

Rows 1–8 present the changes in the schooling gaps when the variable named in the left-hand column is adjusted to the white level while holding the other variables fixed at sample values. The number in column 1 and row 1 of panel A, for example, shows that if the four components of family background listed in rows 1a through 1d are adjusted for blacks to white levels, then the black rate of completing

---

26. Two other problems that past researchers have generally ignored are also solved in our framework. First is the issue of time-varying explanatory variables, such as indicators of the state of the labor market. Previous frameworks are fundamentally atemporal and accommodate variables that change over time only in arbitrary ways. Second, we control for unobserved characteristics. Our framework builds on the work of Cameron and Heckman 1998a: serious biases in the estimated effects of family income on schooling arise when unobserved variables are not accounted for.

TABLE 5-4
CHANGES IN THE WHITE-MINORITY SCHOOLING GAP WITH MINORITY VARIABLES EQUATED TO WHITE LEVELS

	Without AFQT Score		With AFQT Score	
	Blacks	Hispanics	Blacks	Hispanics
A. Probability of being in grade 9 or higher at age 15				
Equating all family background components (1)	.07 (.021)[a]	.08 (.022)[a]	.03 (.022)	.02 (.021)
Individual components				
Number of siblings (1a)	.03 (.009)[a]	.03 (.012)[a]	.02 (.010)[a]	.01 (.013)
Highest grade of father (1b)	.04 (.021)[a]	−.01 (.028)	.01 (.022)	−.03 (.029)
Highest grade of mother (1c)	.01 (.005)[a]	.06 (.021)[a]	.00 (.007)	.04 (.023)[a]
Broken home (1d)	−.02 (.010)	−.003 (.006)	.001 (.010)	.003 (.007)
Equating family income (2)	.09 (.021)[a]	.12 (.021)[a]	.08 (.027)[a]	.04 (.020)[a]
Equating local average wages (3)	−.001 (.002)	.01 (.005)[a]	−.002 (.002)	.008 (.004)[a]
Equating tuition and college proximity (4)	−.01 (.005)[a]	−.02 (.008)[a]	−.02 (.006)[a]	−.02 (.009)[a]

Equating AFQT scores (5)	na	na	.16 (.034)[a]	.17 (.027)[a]
Equating 1 and 2 (6)	.14 (.023)[a]	.18 (.030)[a]	.10 (.025)[a]	.06 (.028)[a]
Equating 1, 2, 3, and 4 (7)	.13 (.021)[a]	.17 (.021)[a]	.08 (.023)[a]	.05 (.027)[a]
Equating 1, 2, 3, 4, and 5 (8)	na	na	.21 (.027)[a]	.20 (.026)[a]
Gap between whites and minorities (9)	.16	.21	.16	.21

B. Probability of high school completion at age 24, high school graduation and GED attainment combined

Equating all family background components (1)	.06 (.014)[a]	.05 (.021)[a]	.03 (.015)[a]	−.01 (.024)
Individual components (1)				
Number of siblings (1a)	.02 (.007)[a]	.03 (.010)[a]	.01 (.007)[a]	.01 (.010)
Highest grade of father (1b)	.03 (.015)[a]	−.01 (.032)	.02 (.016)	−.04 (.029)[a]
Highest grade of mother (1c)	.01 (.005)	.03 (.020)	−.002 (.005)	.02 (.022)
Broken home (1d)	.01 (.008)	−.005 (.006)	.007 (.007)	−.001 (.005)
Equating family income (2)	.07 (.016)[a]	.08 (.018)[a]	.05 (.018)[a]	.01 (.019)

(Table continues)

TABLE 5-4 (continued)

	Without AFQT Score		With AFQT Score	
	Blacks	Hispanics	Blacks	Hispanics
Equating local average wages (3)	.01 (.004)[a]	.01 (.010)	.008 (.004)[a]	.01 (.010)
Equating tuition and college proximity (4)	−.004 (.003)	.006 (.009)	−.007 (.002)[a]	.007 (.008)
Equating AFQT scores (5)	na	na	.11 (.019)[a]	.16 (.019)[a]
Equating 1 and 2 (6)	.12 (.013)	.12 (.021)[a]	.06 (.016)[a]	.002 (.026)
Equating 1, 2, 3, and 4 (7)	.12 (.013)	.13 (.023)[a]	.06 (.017)[a]	.008 (.030)
Equating 1, 2, 3, 4, and 5 (8)	na	na	.15 (.014)[a]	.16 (.026)[a]
Gap between whites and minorities (9)	.08	.14	.08	.14
C. College-entry probabilities at age 24, conditional on high school completion				
Equating all family background components (1)	.10 (.027)[a]	.11 (.026)[a]	.08 (.021)[a]	.05 (.014)[a]
Individual components				
Number of siblings (1a)	.03 (.012)[a]	.03 (.012)[a]	.02 (.011)[a]	.01 (.009)

Highest grade of father (1b)	.08 (.028)[a]	.03 (.032)	.06 (.020)[a]	.02 (.029)
Highest grade of mother (1c)	.003 (.008)	.05 (.025)[a]	−.005 (.006)	.02 (.022)
Broken home (1d)	−.01 (.011)	.01 (.009)	−.002 (.009)	.01 (.008)[a]
Equating family income (2)	.05 (.023)[a]	.03 (.013)[a]	.004 (.020)	−.02 (.019)
Equating local average wages (3)	.004 (.006)	.04 (.013)[a]	.002 (.003)	.03 (.012)[a]
Equating tuition and college proximity (4)	−.03 (.006)[a]	−.05 (.016)[a]	−.02 (.004)[a]	−.05 (.016)[a]
Equating AFQT scores (5)	na	na	.15 (.028)[a]	.12 (.022)[a]
Equating 1 and 2 (6)	.14 (.027)[a]	.13 (.023)[a]	.08 (.027)[a]	.03 (.023)
Equating 1, 2, 3, and 4 (7)	.12 (.029)[a]	.12 (.030)[a]	.06 (.028)[a]	.01 (.030)
Equating 1, 2, 3, 4, and 5 (8)	na	na	.21 (.029)[a]	.13 (.030)[a]
Gap between whites and minorities (9)	.11	.07	.11	.07
D. College-entry probabilities at age 24, unconditional on high school graduation				
Equating all family background components (1)	.13 (.027)[a]	.11 (.026)[a]	.07 (.022)[a]	.03 (.026)

(*Table continues*)

TABLE 5–4 (continued)

	Without AFQT Score		With AFQT Score	
	Blacks	Hispanics	Blacks	Hispanics
Individual components				
Number of siblings (1a)	.04	.04	.02	.01
	(.011)[a]	(.013)[a]	(.010)[a]	(.012)
Highest grade of father (1b)	.09	.017	.06	−.01
	(.026)[a]	(.021)	(.020)[a]	(.026)
Highest grade of mother (1c)	.005	.055	−.005	.02
	(.008)	(.028)[a]	(.006)	(.023)
Broken home (1d)	−.004	−.009	.003	.01
	(.011)	(.007)	(.010)	(.007)
Equating family income (2)	.08	.06	.03	−.007
	(.023)[a]	(.210)[a]	(.022)	(.018)

Equating local average wages (3)	.008 (.004)[a]	.03 (.013)[a]	.003 (.005)	.02 (.013)
Equating tuition and college proximity (4)	−.03 (.006)[a]	−.03 (.015)[a]	−.02 (.005)[a]	−.04 (.013)[a]
Equating AFQT scores (5)	na	na	.18 (.029)[a]	.19 (.023)[a]
Equating 1 through 2 (6)	.19 (.027)[a]	.17 (.030)[a]	.11 (.028)[a]	.03 (.028)[a]
Equating 1 through 4 (7)	.16 (.029)[a]	.17 (.032)[a]	.09 (.029)[a]	.01 (.030)
Equating 1 through 5 (8)	na	na	.27 (.033)[a]	.21 (.035)[a]
Gap between whites and minorities (9)	.12	.14	.12	.14

NOTE: The simulations were calculated by shifting the mean of the explanatory variables for minorities to the mean of the variables for whites. For example, the number in row 2 of panel D represents the rise in college entry if each black family were given an income transfer equal to the mean difference in black and white family incomes. Standard errors are in parentheses.
a. Significant at the 10 percent level.
SOURCE: Cameron and Heckman (1998b), based on NLSY data 1979–1989.

ninth grade rises by seven percentage points. In adjusting for these factors, blacks would have a ninth-grade completion rate at age fifteen, only nine percentage points lower than the white rate rather than the sixteen percentage point gap actually found in the data.[27] Rows 1a–1d show the change in the gap when the individual components of family background are equated (see table 5–3 for definitions and group means). Row 2 shows the change when minority family income is adjusted to white levels, and row 3 displays the same change when county average wages are equalized. Next, row 4 shows the effect of adjusting tuition and college proximity, and row 5 shows the effect of equalizing ability. Finally, rows 6–8 show combined effects of various incremental simulations. Columns 1 and 2 show the predicted gap between whites and blacks and whites and Hispanics, respectively. Columns 3 and 4 report the corresponding calculations when the AFQT score is included in the set of explanatory variables to proxy long-term family and environmental influences.

From columns 1 and 2 in each panel, we reach several important conclusions. First, row 2 shows that adjusting for family income alone reduces the white-minority gaps in high school completion substantially and some gap in college entry. This confirms the univariate analysis of the preceding subsection. For high school completion, the white-black gap would completely vanish as would most of the white-Hispanic gap (compare rows 2 and 9). A similar conclusion holds for college entry (panel D), though the effect is not quite as dramatic. Adjusting family income raises black and Hispanic college enrollment eight and six percentage points, respectively. The actual gaps are twelve and fourteen, respectively.

Before concluding that family income is the whole story or even the main story in explaining minority-white schooling differences, it is important to notice rows 1a–1d, which show that long-term family background differences play a more powerful role than family income

---

27. In these simulations, only the means of the variables are equated between the two groups. Consider the adjustment for sibling size. This is accomplished by finding the difference in the mean number of siblings between blacks and whites (see table 5–3 for exact values) and then forming predicted black high school completion probabilities after subtracting that difference from each black person in the sample. Thus, the rise in black schooling due to a decrease in the number of siblings (family size) is reported in the table. Because these models are nonlinear, there are other ways of making these simulations, such as using the marginal distributions of white attributes but preserving the original covariance structure. These more elaborate methods have little impact on the simulations. We report the simplest and most easily replicable results.

in explaining minority-majority differences in grade attainment, especially for the transition to college among high school graduates (panel C) and for total college entry (panel D). The effects of equating family background (holding family income and other explanatory variables constant) are particularly strong for attending college (panel D). For blacks and Hispanics, they explain, respectively, thirteen and eleven percentage points of the twelve and fourteen percentage point gaps.[28] For both college enrollment measures, adjusting for family background and family income (row 6) more than explains the minority-majority gaps. Such adjustments nearly explain the high school gap. Family background and income are the main determinants of all four attainment statuses that we study. Other variables explain little of the white-minority schooling gaps.

Local labor market variables representing the opportunities available to persons with little education are statistically significant in our estimated model but play only a modest role in explaining schooling continuation decisions. They contribute little to explaining white-minority differences (row 3). The reason is that average differences in local labor market conditions among the groups are small (see the means in table 5–3).

Equating tuition and college proximity (row 4) *increases* the white-minority gap for college entry (both unconditional and for high school graduates) and high school completion although the effects are only substantial for college entry.[29] The reason, as revealed by the means in table 5–3, is that blacks and Hispanics face lower average tuition and have more geographic proximity to college than whites. Equating minority to white levels *lowers* college participation for blacks and Hispanics.

Columns 3 and 4 repeat the same simulation exercises when scholastic ability as measured by AFQT is included as an explanatory variable. Comparing the family income and background effects in row 2 when AFQT is in the model (columns 3 and 4) and when it is not demonstrates that the effects of family income for high school comple-

---

28. These adjustments exclude AFQT scores.

29. College tuition and proximity were included in the explanatory variables for high school completion because college entry may be a primary motivator of high school graduation. Thus, higher college costs could lead to lower high school graduation rates. In our joint work, we find little evidence for such an effect. Both tuition and proximity variables are small in magnitude and statistical significance for all groups. For college entry, by contrast, both college tuition and proximity are statistically significant and numerically important for all race groups, though adjustment widens the white-minority gap slightly.

tion, college attendance given completion, and college attendance are substantially weakened by the inclusion of AFQT scores. The change is most dramatic for Hispanics. For this group, estimated family income effects essentially vanish. They are greatly weakened for blacks. Similar effects appear in a less dramatic fashion when family background variables and income are included in the model rather than the more controversial AFQT variable (see row 6). Introducing AFQT into the model also weakens the estimated effect of family income on grade attainment at age fifteen, but the income effects at earlier transitions remain. If family income is interpreted as a measure of short-term credit constraints, it is the constraints *before* the transition to college that play a more powerful role.

Equating family background and income raises Hispanic high school completion and college entry by 12 and 17 percentage points, respectively, when AFQT is not included in the schooling model (see panels B and D). The corresponding reductions in the gaps attributable to these variables when AFQT is included are only 0.2 and 0.03 percentage points, respectively. If minority AFQT alone were adjusted to white levels, then college entry would rise by 18 percentage points for blacks and 19 percentage points for Hispanics (row 5, columns 3 and 4) (see panel D). The college-entry effects from adjusting AFQT for high school completers are 15 and 12 percentage points. There are also strong effects of introducing AFQT on diminishing the role of family income in explaining racial and ethnic gaps in college attendance among high school graduates (see panel C). Regardless of income and family background, at the same AFQT level, blacks and Hispanics enter college at rates that are substantially *higher* than the white rate. The effects of AFQT on predicting high school completion are also dramatic.

The role of AFQT in explaining racial and ethnic schooling differences is important.[30] It is long-run factors that promote scholastic ability that explain most of the measured gaps in college enrollment and not the short-run credit constraints that receive most of the attention

---

30. One problem with the AFQT score in these data is that the test was taken in 1980, while the sample was still of high school age. Thus, because AFQT is both a cause and a consequence of schooling, causal statements are difficult. Cameron and Heckman 1998a addresses this problem econometrically and finds little difference in the estimated results when account is taken of the endogeneity. For college-entry decisions, however, the test was taken before virtually all of the sample had reached the age of college entry, so the causal influence of this variable is more clear-cut. Our sample is for persons thirteen to sixteen when they took the AFQT test so none entered college and few graduated from high school. AFQT measures we use are age adjusted.

TABLE 5–5
EFFECTS OF $10,000 INCREASE IN FAMILY INCOME ON COLLEGE ENTRY
OF HIGH SCHOOL GRADUATES AND GED HOLDERS BY
TYPE OF COLLEGE FIRST ATTENDED

	Whites	Blacks	Hispanics
A. Combined two- and four-year college effect			
Excluding AFQT	.018[a]	.032[a]	.016[a]
	(.006)	(.012)	(.008)
Including AFQT	.008	.005	−.012
	(.006)	(.012)	(.013)
B. Two-year and four-year effects excluding AFQT			
Two-year college	−.002	.008	.005
	(.005)	(.008)	(.005)
Four-year college	.020[a]	.024[a]	.011[a]
	(.005)	(.008)	(.004)
C. Two-year and four-year effects including AFQT			
Two-year college	−.003	−.002	−.008
	(.005)	(.008)	(.007)
Four-year college	.010[a]	.007	−.004
	(.005)	(.008)	(.010)

NOTE: Standard errors are in parentheses.
a. Significant at the 10 percent level.
SOURCE: Cameron and Heckman (1998b); NLSY 1979–1989.

in popular public discussion. If short-term family income plays any role at all, it is in high school dropout decisions.

Table 5–5 states the major findings just reported in a different way. Rather than showing how schooling gaps change in response to adjustments in the explanatory variables, it shows the predicted change in schooling attainment in response to a substantial $10,000 rise in family income on college entry for each racial-ethnic group, both with and without AFQT included in the estimating equations.[31] Comparing rows 1 and 2 of panel A shows that family-income effects of college enrollment are reduced to about one-third of their size when AFQT is

31. These results do not condition on high school graduation and include the effect of family income on increasing educational attainment at all ages.

included in the model. (Similar results are found for the college enrollment effect not conditioning on high school graduation.)

Panels B and C of the table make an additional point. Even when AFQT is not included among the explanatory variables, family income is only a trivial determinant of two-year college entry.[32] Thus, comparing rows 3 and 4 of the table reveals that the measured effect of family income is largely due to its effect on four-year entry and not to its effect on two-year college entry. Including AFQT among the explanatory variables (panel C) does not reverse this conclusion; it only weakens the estimated effect of family income on four-year college entry. This evidence reveals that, controlling for ability, the estimated relationship between income and college entry is mainly a relationship between income and entry into four-year college. There is virtually no effect of changes in family income on enrollment into two-year schools.

The Effects of College Tuition. We next use our estimates to examine how tuition levels and Pell grants affect two- and four-year enrollments. Table 5–6 shows the effects of a $1,000 increase in tuition on college-entry probabilities. To be consistent with the received literature, these simulations are performed only for high school graduates.[33] A baseline set of estimates for each race group is shown in row 1. The estimates are for entry at two- and four-year colleges combined. The effects for whites, blacks, and Hispanics are shown in columns 1, 2, and 3, respectively. These estimates are close to the median estimate (after an inflation-adjustment) presented by Leslie and Brinkman (1986) in their survey of more than twenty studies of the effects of tuition on college enrollment.[34]

---

32. Differential tuition costs between two- and four-year schools along with the other variables mentioned above are held constant in these simulations.

33. The table shows how high school graduates would respond to changes in tuition policy. As noted, college tuition has a negligible influence on secondary school completion choices. The results for college entry not conditioning on high school graduation are similar to the estimates reported in the text and, for the sake of brevity, are not reported.

34. In results presented in Cameron and Heckman (1998b), we check the robustness of the baseline estimates. State tuition levels may be correlated with unobserved differences in state-specific factors that explain enrollment due to budget constraints or political pressure by interest groups. Ideally, one would like to control for state effects and tuition effects in the same analysis. Given the limited variation in the state tuition policies over our sample period, we cannot effect such controls. As an alternative, we use controls for region. The addition of dummy variables indicating region reduces the estimated effects by 20–30 percent.

TABLE 5–6

EFFECTS OF $1,000 INCREASE IN GROSS TUITION ON COLLEGE-ENTRY
PROBABILITIES OF HIGH SCHOOL GRADUATES AND GED HOLDERS BY
FAMILY-INCOME QUARTILE AND BY AFQT QUARTILE

	Whites	Blacks	Hispanics
A. Gross tuition effects[a]			
No explanatory variables except tuition in the model	−.17	−.10	−.10
Baseline specification (see note at table base, includes family income, background, and so forth)	−.06	−.04	−.06
Adding AFQT to the row 2 specification	−.05	−.03	−.06
B. Family-income quartiles (baseline)			
Top quartile	−.04	−.01	−.04
Second quartile	−.06	−.03	−.05
Third quartile	−.07	−.07	−.08
Bottom quartile	−.06	−.05	−.08
Joint test of equal effects across quartiles (P-values)	.49	.23	.66
C. Family-income quartiles (baseline plus AFQT)			
Top quartile	−.02	−.02	−.02
Second quartile	−.06	.00	−.05
Third quartile	−.07	−.05	−.09
Bottom quartile	−.04	−.04	−.07
Joint test of equal effects across quartiles (P-values)	.34	.45	.49
D. AFQT quartiles (AFQT plus tuition-AFQT interaction terms)			
Top quartile	−.03	−.02	−.03
Second quartile	−.06	−.01	−.05
Third quartile	−.06	−.03	−.07
Bottom quartile	−.05	−.03	−.05
Joint test of equal effects across quartiles (P-values)	.60	.84	.68

NOTES: These simulations assume both two-year and four-year college tuition increase by $1,000 for the population of high school completers. The baseline specification used in row 2 and rows 4–7 includes controls for family background, family income, average wages in the local labor market, tuition at local colleges, controls for urban and southern residence, tuition–family income interactions, estimated Pell grant award eligibility, and dummy variables, that indicate the proximity of two- and four-year colleges. Definitions of the variables are located in table 5–3. The panel D specification adds AFQT and an AFQT-tuition interaction to the baseline specification.
a. Gross tuition is the nominal sticker-price of college and excludes scholarship and loan support.
SOURCE: Cameron and Heckman (1998b); NLSY data, 1979–1989.

Including family background variables (as defined in tables 5-3 and 5-7) greatly diminishes the estimated effect of tuition on schooling. Adding AFQT further weakens the estimated effect. Nonetheless, the effects of tuition on enrollment are substantial, even with AFQT controlled. Given the pattern of a smaller black response to tuition, however, recent tuition increases *reduce* black-white differences in college enrollment. The more negative estimates for Hispanics account for only a small component of the difference between Hispanic and white college enrollment rates. Cameron and Heckman (1998b) report that the estimated effect of the tuition increase operates through its effect on attendance at community colleges. There is essentially no effect of college tuition increases on enrollment in four-year schools.

Panel B shows how estimated responses to tuition vary by family income quartile.[35] For each demographic group, the top quartile is much less responsive to tuition increases than are the other quartiles although these effects are never statistically significantly different from the tuition effects for other quartiles for each demographic group using conventional significance levels. Such differences in response to tuition by income class have been noted in the literature (Kane in this volume) and have been interpreted as evidence that low-income persons are more responsive to tuition because of borrowing constraints. One cannot, however, reject the hypothesis that the tuition coefficients are the same across income classes for each demographic group. With ability controlled, the estimated effects of tuition on enrollment diminish, especially for blacks (see the estimates reported in panel C). Again, one cannot reject the null of equality of the coefficients on tuition across income quartiles. Panel D reports the response to the tuition increase across AFQT quartiles. For all demographic groups, one cannot reject the hypothesis of equality of the estimated effects of tuition on first enrollment into college.

Table 5-7 tests one commonly stated version of the credit-constraint hypothesis. It postulates that if students are severely credit constrained and family income limits their attendance, a $1,000 rise in tuition should have equal and opposite effects on schooling decisions as a $1,000 rise in family income. The estimated effects of family income on schooling are an order of magnitude smaller than the estimated effects of tuition when AFQT is excluded from the model. When AFQT is included, estimated family-income effects decline further by a factor of three-four while estimated tuition effects are barely affected. When AFQT is excluded, for whites and Hispanics one can de-

---

35. These numbers are calculated from a model that included income-tuition interaction terms.

TABLE 5–7
P-VALUES OF CHI-SQUARE TEST OF EQUAL MAGNITUDE OF $1,000
RISE IN TUITION AND $1,000 RISE IN FAMILY INCOME

	Whites	Blacks	Hispanics
Excluding AFQT			
$1,000 rise in family income	.0028	.0035	.0026
	(.0009)	(.0012)	(.0011)
$1,000 rise in tuition	−.06	−.04	−.06
	(.02)	(.02)	(.03)
P-values of equality test	.02	.08	.03
Including AFQT			
$1,000 rise in family income	.0009	.0008	−.001
	(.007)	(.002)	(.001)
$1,000 rise in tuition	−.05	−.03	−.06
	(.02)	(.02)	(.04)
P-values of equality test	.07	.18	.08

NOTE: Standard errors of estimates in parentheses.
SOURCE: Cameron and Heckman (1998b); NLSY, 1979–1989.

cisively reject the hypothesis of equality of the effects at conventional significance levels. For blacks, the hypothesis is rejected at the 10 percent level. When AFQT is included, the estimated family-income effects become so imprecisely determined that one cannot reject the hypothesis of equality although the point estimates are dramatically different. The estimated income effects are numerically small. The key result driving this inference is that family-income effects are not statistically significantly different from zero. Tuition and family income play fundamentally different roles in college attendance decisions. This evidence is consistent with the absence of credit constraints.

Cameron and Heckman 1998b also examines the effect of changes in Pell grant schedules on enrollment in college. Our analysis and the analyses of other researchers (see chapter 4) find little evidence of changes in estimated Pell grant benefits on enrollment in college. A $1,000 increase in Pell grant entitlements produces less than a 1 percent increase in enrollments as opposed to about a 6–8 percent response from a comparable change in tuition. Pell grants should offset tuition costs for low-income people and should have effects of equal but opposite magnitude on college enrollment.

Orfield (1992) and Kane (this volume) postulate that poor people may not have reliable information about their own Pell grant eligibility. This can account for the disparity in response to tuition rates and potential scholarship rates. Heckman, Smith, and Wittekind (1997) show that, among persons eligible for the Job Training Partnership Act program targeted toward the poor, the poorest and least educated are less likely to be aware of Pell grants. Thus, family background factors play a substantial role in making prospective students aware of their Pell grant benefits. It seems unlikely, however, that the magnitude of this informational deficit can explain the estimated 8 to 1 discrepancy in the estimated price effects. It does not seem plausible that children of poor persons who have persevered through high school would be unaware of their eligibility for grants and loans. It seems more likely that able and college-ready students are aware of their eligibility for grants and act on the information. Indeed, Heckman, Smith, and Wittekind find that low-income high school graduates are much more aware of their eligibility for Pell grant programs than are high school dropouts, and their awareness rate is about 60 percent. This high level of reported awareness makes it unlikely that the Orfield explanation is the whole story or even the main story for why the response rate to Pell grants is so low compared with the response to tuition.[36]

Supporting Evidence from Other Studies

Shea's (1996) analysis provides mild support for our analysis. He argues that, to identify the contribution of credit constraints to schooling choice, one needs to look at how unexpected changes in family income influence educational attainment and hence the earnings of children. Using the Panel Study of Income Dynamics data, he estimates the correlation between children's income and variations in the father's labor income due to predictable and unpredictable components. (An instance of the latter is job loss through plant shutdown; an instance of the former is the father's education.) Shea finds that predictable components of family income are positively correlated with the child's income, but components of family income due to "luck" are uncorrelated with the child's income. He finds no evidence that increases in

---

36. The log odds ratio of a high school graduate with no college education being aware of the Pell grant program is twice as great as the log odds ratio for a high school dropout. The Orfield argument might be salvaged by claiming that persons who were unaware of Pell grants in high school failed to graduate because they were unaware of the grants.

unpredictable components affect children's income, and hence he finds no evidence in support of credit constraints.[37]

Other, though indirect, evidence is provided by Altonji and Dunn (1996). If short-term credit constraints do not hinder college entry and access to credit markets is available to everyone, there should be no relation between the returns to education and family income, provided consumption motives for schooling are unimportant. Once a student graduates from high school, he should invest until the return from another dollar spent on education is the same as the return on physical assets. Altonji and Dunn find that rates of return are more or less constant across individuals and do not vary systematically by family income.[38] Thus, their evidence supports evidence reported in table 5–4 that short-run credit market constraints are not a significant determinant of schooling and college choices.

The research of Duncan, Brooks-Gunn, Yeung, and Smith (1998) supports our general argument. Using data from the Panel Survey of Income Dynamics, they report that completed schooling (and other measures of child well-being) are much more strongly related to family income in early childhood than to income at later years.

Another piece of evidence comes from Cameron and Heckman (1998a), who analyze the determinants of grade-by-grade schooling attainment for five cohorts of American males. While policy makers and economists have focused on the measured effects of family income on college entry, Cameron and Heckman find that family-income and family background factors are powerful determinants of choices at all stages of the schooling process, from the decision to complete elementary school through entry into graduate school. There is a stable behavioral relationship between family background and schooling continuation across all levels of schooling, from elementary school through entry into graduate school. When, however, they condition on AFQT, the effect of family income on college attendance declines and becomes numerically smaller and statistically insignificant. Analysts who have studied only the relationship between college choice and family income have ignored the fact that family income and other measures of family background, such as parental education, are also strong

---

37. A major problem with Shea's analysis is that he does not justify which components of family income are predictable and which are not. In addition, he does not separate the effects of luck on younger children from the effects on older children. His evidence suggests that unexpected lottery winnings would have no effect on schooling choices regardless of their time of arrival.

38. If there were a strong consumption motive for education, the rate of return to schooling should be lower for children from higher-income families.

determinants of decisions to complete the ninth grade and to attend and graduate from high school where tuition costs are effectively zero. No appeal to borrowing constraints is required to explain the relationship between family income and college attendance decisions.

The importance of family background in determining educational choices is found in other policy environments and other countries as well. The collection of papers in Blossfeld and Shavit (1993) studies data from a variety of countries in different stages of political and economic development with profoundly different institutional organizations for education. They document roughly the same basic pattern found in the U.S. data: family background and family income are important determinants of schooling choices from the earliest grade levels to the highest, regardless of whether college tuition costs paid by students are large or small.

General Equilibrium Effects

Thus far we followed the tradition in the educational policy literature and have ignored the effects of tuition change instituted by a national policy. In response to a nationally instituted tuition policy, more persons enroll in college, and the price of skills declines as college-educated labor becomes less scarce. If prospective students anticipate this labor market adjustment and respond appropriately and if the effects of taxes raised to finance such a policy are accounted for using an approximation to the current U.S. tax system, the estimated effects of tuition on college enrollment are considerably diminished.

Heckman, Lochner, and Taber (1998a, b) develop an overlapping-generations model of skill formation with heterogeneous agents that extends the analysis of Auerbach and Kotlikoff by including two skills that are chosen by agents who differ in ability. When a revenue-neutral tuition subsidy is simulated with their model, they find that the general equilibrium tuition elasticity is about *ten times* smaller than what is estimated with the standard cross-sectional methodology described by Kane in his contribution to this volume and reported in this chapter.

In a world with rational agents, tuition and all forgone earnings of college students would have to be subsidized, and a substantial bonus payment to students would have to be paid to those who attend college to induce them to undertake the 80 percent increase in the annual supply of college equivalents required to eliminate the college–high school wage differential. This would require an unprecedented level of subsidy that would be unlikely to receive political support in the current environment of fiscal stringency. A feasible national tuition policy can go only a small way toward alleviating wage inequality in the modern economy.

The evidence reported in Heckman, Lochner, and Taber (1998a) suggests that, in the current environment, skill prices movements alone will induce a sufficient supply response to eliminate rising wage inequality. No tuition policy is required. Tuition policy will, at best, shorten the transition time to the stage of lower inequality, but the effects on the transition are slight.

To the extent that income and tuition subsidies promote college attendance, some additional evidence reported by Cameron and Heckman (1998a) is worth mentioning. Students induced into college attendance and graduation by government policies—the marginal students—are of lower quality than those already attending college. The labor market returns to a college education for a marginal student will be smaller than those for the average college graduate. By failing to distinguish between the marginal and the average student, current policy discussions also offer an overly optimistic account of what tuition policy can accomplish in raising the income of the newly educated.

Likely Impact of the Hope Tax Credit

We have conducted a simulation of the recently enacted Hope tax credit. In this volume, Kane provides a comprehensive discussion of this program. The simulation uses the estimates of enrollment response presented by Cameron and Heckman (1998b) to answer two questions. First, with other factors constant, what is the predicted enrollment response to the program? Second, how much of the cost of the program will go to families whose children would have gone to college without the program? The main feature of the program is a tax credit of up to $1,500 for two years of college. We use the estimates from row 2 of table 5–6 (no AFQT and no region controls but with family background, local labor market variables, and other characteristics). This is the traditional specification used in the literature.

Even with the large increases in the real price of public colleges in the United States over the past fifteen years, average annual tuition rates are still relatively low: $1,283 for two-year college and $2,986 at four-year schools. The estimated enrollment response to the Hope program is a 4.2 percentage point increase in two-year enrollments and a 0.9 percentage point decrease in four-year enrollments (3.3 increase for both categories combined). Thus, most response to the program comes in the form of enrollment in two-year schools. At least 91 percent of the cost of this program will be spent on people who would enter college in the absence of the program.[39]

Summary and Implications for Educational Policy

This chapter examines the evidence on three issues. First, tuition reduction policies that are feasible are unlikely to have much effect on wage inequality. Second, we consider whether short-term borrowing constraints impede college attendance The strong correlation between college attendance and family resources is widely interpreted as evidence that constraints on short-term borrowing impede enrollment. We argue that their importance is greatly exaggerated. The long-term influence of family income and family background as captured by our measure of ability or by parental education explains best the correlation. Family income matters, but its greatest influence is on forming the ability and college-readiness of children and not in financing college education.

Third, this chapter examines racial-ethnic differences in schooling. We find that with family background controlled, minorities are more likely than whites to graduate from high school and to attend college. Again, long-term factors account for this relationship, not short-term cash constraints that can be fixed by Pell grants or Hope tax credits offered to children late in their life cycle of adolescent development.

We raise a number of questions about the empirical and intellectual foundations of current government income-subsidy programs designed to promote college attendance. The edifice in place is generous to minorities and to children from poor families. A main conclusion from our work is that, to raise college attendance and improve the prospects for success in college, policy should focus on ensuring that more students graduate from high school and obtain the skills and motivation required to perform successful college work. Government policies such as Pell grants and other tuition subsidies focus on getting high school graduates into college, but our evidence suggests that the scope for such policies is minimal because most of the problem of disparity in schooling attainment among racial, ethnic, and income groups arises at earlier points in the life cycle of children from poor families.

---

39. Details of the Hope tax credits are given in chapter 4 in this volume. The enrollment predictions are based on tuition estimates presented in panel B of table 5–6 (controlling for family income but not for AFQT). To simplify the calculation of the enrollment response, the tax credit is assumed to vanish if family income is above $80,000 per year.

Appendix A
Problems with the CPS Data

Influential studies by Hauser (1991) and Kane (1994) use data from the Current Population Survey (CPS) to investigate the role of tuition costs, financial aid, family background, and family income in explaining the time series of black-white college attendance. A major problem with using these data to correlate family income with college entry is that young persons who do not live at home and who do not live in group quarters (that is, dormitories if they attend college) are assigned their own income in the survey rather than that of their parents. This limitation has given rise to a convention in the CPS-based determinants of schooling literature: estimating the determinants of college entry on samples restricted to dependent children who are high school graduates. It also gives rise to a focus on college enrollment rather than on college graduation despite the greater importance of the latter in determining career outcomes. The CPS dependency link between youths and their parents becomes much weaker for youths making postsecondary schooling decisions beyond initial entry decisions since it is unusual for students to stay at home for many years after leaving high school.

This convention creates two distinct problems: (1) excluding nondependents means that the sample is no longer random and may not represent family-income effects on schooling participation for the population more generally and (2) statistical problems arise because the factors that influence the decision to live as a dependent may also govern college attendance decisions.[40] All said, CPS analysts underestimate (in absolute value) the effect of variables that promote schooling on schooling attainment because any variable, such as family income, that moves college attendance and dependency status together will likely overstate (in absolute value) the true effect. If higher family income, for example, is associated with both higher dependency and higher college attendance by children, then the estimated effect of family income on college attendance will be smaller than the true population effect if one only studies samples of dependents.

Cameron and Heckman 1992 demonstrates the impact of this measurement problem on estimating the impact of family income on

---

40. Conditioning on a choice variable (dependency status) generates a potential simultaneous equations problem since dependency status likely is affected by the same unobservables governing college attendance decisions. By using dependency as a conditioning variable, CPS analysts likely produce biased estimates of the impact of socioeconomic variables on college attendance.

college attendance and show that strong effects of family income are obscured by this convention, particularly for blacks.

Appendix B
Racial and Ethnic Differences in Family Background, Ability, and Access to Schooling and Tuition

The means of the variables used in the multivariate analysis are defined at the base of table 5–3. Variables are divided into five basic categories and include the following: (1) family environmental variables (parental education, whether the person lived with both parents at age fourteen), (2) family resources (family income and the number of siblings), (3) the attractiveness of nonschooling alternatives (wages in unskilled and semiskilled industries measured in the individual's county of residence), (4) college costs (tuition, college proximity—whether a college exists in the county of residence—and Pell grant aid schedules as summarized by average amounts), and (5) scholastic ability (AFQT). Two additional variables—whether the individual lived in a southern state and whether the person lived in an urban area—are also included in the list to be consistent with many previous studies though it is difficult to be precise about the meaning of these variables on schooling decisions.

Comparing the means in table 5–3 across groups shows sizable differences in family background characteristics among blacks, Hispanics, and whites. Family size is much larger for blacks and Hispanics than for whites.[41] Parental education is lowest for Hispanics and highest for whites. Family income is lowest for blacks, almost 20 percent higher for Hispanics, and about 50 percent larger when whites are compared with blacks. Broken homes are much more prevalent among blacks and least prevalent among whites: only 13 percent of whites lived in a broken home at age fourteen compared to 27 percent for Hispanics and a sizable 43 percent of blacks.

County local labor market conditions, by contrast, vary little among the groups. Average county unemployment rates, measured at age eighteen when most people finish high school, were in fact lowest for blacks at 6 percent and highest for Hispanics at 6.9 percent, with whites in between at 6.3 percent. Average county wages in industries with concentrations of unskilled and low-skilled jobs also varied little,

---

41. All the family sizes overstate the U.S. population averages because the sampling frame in the NLSY is size-biased on family size. See Rao (1965) for a discussion of size-biased sampling.

though they were, in fact, lowest for whites at $18,000 and highest for Hispanics at $19,900.

The next set of means shows that college costs and college proximity favor minority college entry. Since we are interested in any college rather than entry into a specific college, we use measures of tuition that will best reflect whether a person goes to college at all. In particular, if available, we use a tuition measure constructed for two- and four-year public colleges located in the county of residence. Since there is only small variation in the county-level measures compared with state-level tuition measures (which are measured as enrollment-weighted averages across all public institutions in a given state), the table reports two- and four-year averages at the state level and the two-year tuition for the county in which the person lives at age eighteen for completeness. (In the analysis of Cameron and Heckman (1998b), tuition is allowed to vary by age to capture year-to-year differences in college costs that may influence college entry.) Regardless of how tuition is measured, Hispanics face the lowest tuition charges and whites the highest, with blacks falling in between. This finding reflects the fact that, compared with whites, blacks and especially Hispanics are geographically concentrated in states with low-tuition policies.

While the amount of Pell grant aid for which a person is eligible depends on college tuition, we show only the imputed size of the Pell grant award if the person went to the local four-year school. This measure shows important variation among groups. Hispanics and blacks are eligible for the largest awards—$1,210 and $1,154, respectively—and whites the lowest at $501. Taken together, an average white male going to four-year college would need to cover $1,200 in college tuition through his own contribution or some other form of aid, while the average black and Hispanic male would need to cover $414 and $180, respectively.[42]

Another important component of the cost of college is proximity to a school. Students may have an easier time covering transportation costs and providing room and board at home than paying for board and room at a college dorm. College proximity measures the existence of either a two- or four-year college in the county of residence. Again, college proximity favors black and Hispanic college entry. Hispanics and blacks have a 92 and 89 percent proximity rate, respectively, while whites face a rate of 82 percent, which by any measure is still high.

We use AFQT scores as a measure of scholastic ability. The white-

---

42. These tuition values are for the sample period 1979–1989 and are expressed in 1994 dollars. For both reasons they do not match the tuition figures for 1994–1997 discussed in the text.

minority differences are large and statistically significant. The average Hispanic falls in the middle, and the average white has the highest score. The gap between whites and Hispanics is large and significant, as is the gap between Hispanics and blacks.

References

Altonji, J., and T. Dunn. 1996. "Returns to Education and the Family." *Review of Economics and Statistics* 128 (4): 692–704.

Blossfeld, H., and Y. Shavit. 1993. *Persistent Inequality: Changing Educational Attainment in Thirteen Countries.* Boulder: Westview Press.

Browning, M., J. Heckman, and L. Hansen. 1999. In *Handbook of Macroeconomics,* edited by J. Taylor and M. Woodford. North Holland: Amsterdam.

Callan, P. 1997. "Stewards of Opportunity: American Public Community Colleges." *Daedalus* 126 (4): 95–112.

Cameron, S. V., and J. Heckman. 1998a. "Life Cycle Schooling and Educational Selectivity: Models and Choice." *Journal of Political Economy* 106 (2) (April).

———. 1998b. "The Dynamics of Education Attainment for Blacks, Whites, and Hispanics." University of Chicago.

———. 1994. "The Determinants of High School Graduation and College Attendance." In *Training and the Private Sector,* edited by Lisa M. Lynch. Chicago: University of Chicago Press.

———. 1993. "The Nonequivalence of High School Equivalents." *Journal of Labor Economics* 11 (January): 1–47.

———. 1992. "Comment on Hauser." In *Studies of Supplies and Demand in Higher Education,* edited by Charles Clotfelter and Michael Rothschild, 105–19. Chicago: University of Chicago Press.

Clotfelter, C., R. Ehrenberg, M. Getz, and J. J. Siegfried. 1991: *Economic Challenges in Higher Education.* Chicago: University of Chicago Press.

College Board. 1997. "Trends in Student Aid: 1986–1996." Washington, D.C.: College Board.

Duncan, Greg, Jeanne Brooks-Gunn, W. Jean Yeung, and Judith Smith. 1998. "How Much Does Childhood Poverty Affect the Life Chances of Children?" *American Sociological Review* 63 (June): 406–23.

Hansen, L. 1983. "Impact of Student Financial Aid on Access." In *The Crisis in Higher Education,* edited by Joseph Froomkin. New York: Academy of Political Science.

Hauser, R. 1993. "Trends in College Attendance among Blacks, Whites, and Hispanics." In *Studies of Supply and Demand in Higher Education,* edited by C. Clotfelter and M. Rothschild. Chicago: University of Chicago Press.

———. 1991. "The Decline in College Entry among African Americans:

Findings in Search of Explanations." Unpublished manuscript, University of Wisconsin.

Heckman, J., 1995 "Lessons from the Bell Curve." *Journal of Political Economy* 103 (5): 1091–120.

———. 1996. "Should the U.S. Have a Human Capital Policy and If So, What Should It Be?" Gilbert Lecture, University of Rochester.

Heckman, J., L. Lochner, and C. Taber. 1998a. "Explaining Rising Wage Inequality: Explorations with a Dynamic General Equilibrium Model of Earnings with Heterogeneous Agents." *Review of Economic Dynamics* 1 (1): 1–54.

———. 1998b. "General Equilibrium Treatment Effects: A Study of Tuition Policy." *American Economic Review* 88 (2) (May): 381–86.

Heckman, J., J. Smith, and M. Wittekind. 1997. "Awareness of Social Programs." Unpublished manuscript, University of Chicago.

Johnson, G. 1970. "The Demand for Labor by Educational Category." *Southern Economic Journal* 37: 190–204.

Kane, T. 1994. "College Entry by Blacks since 1970: The Role of College Costs, Family Background and the Returns to Education." *Journal of Political Economy* 102: 878–911.

———. 1995. "Rising Public College Tuition and College Entry: How Well Do Public Subsidies Promote Access to College?" NBER working paper 5164.

Kane, T., and C. Rouse. 1995. "The Labor Market Returns to Two and Four Year College: Is a Credit a Credit and Do Degrees Matter?" *American Economic Review* 85 (3): 606–14.

Katz, L., and K. Murphy. 1992. "Changes in Relative Wages, 1963–1987: Supply and Demand Factors." *Quarterly Journal of Economics* 107 (1): 35–78.

Krueger, A. 1997. "What's Up with Wages?" November, Goldman Sachs U.S. Economic Research, pp. 1–18.

Lazear, E. 1977. "Education, Consumption vs. Production?" *Journal of Political Economy* 85 (3): 569–98.

Leslie, M., and L. Brinkman. 1988. *The Economic Value of Higher Education.* New York: Macmillan.

McPherson, M., and M. O. Schapiro. 1991. "Does Student Aid Affect College Enrollment? New Evidence on a Persistent Controversy." *American Economic Review* 81 (1) (March): 309–18.

Mortenson, T. 1988. "Pell Grant Program Changes and Their Effects on Applicant Eligibility." American College Testing Program Research Report 88-2.

National Center for Education Statistics. 1997. *The 1997 Digest of Education Statistics.* Washington, D.C.: NCES.

Orfield, G. 1992. "Money, Equity, and College Access." *Harvard Educational Review* 72 (3) (fall): 337–72.

Rao, C. R. 1965. "On Discrete Distributions Arising out of Methods of Ascertainment." In *Classical and Contagious Discrete Distributions,* edited by G. P. Patil, pp. 320–33. Calcutta: Statistical Publication Society.

Reich, R. 1991. *The Work of Nations: Preparing Ourselves for 21st Century Capitalism.* New York: Knopf.

Shea, J. 1996. "Does Parent's Money Matter?" University of Maryland working paper.

St. John, Edward P. 1993. "Untangling the Web: Using the Price-Response Measures in Enrollment Projections." *Journal of Higher Education* 64 (6) (November/December): 675–95.

Index

Armed Forces Qualification Test (AFQT), 17, 98, 106–10, 110–13, 115, 121–22

Banking industry, 72
Blacks. *See* Ethnic and minority issues
Bush, George, 10–11

California, 59, 65
Clinton, William, 2, 8, 10, 19, 28, 45
Clinton administration, 8, 19, 28, 44–50, 66–68
Cold war, 3
Colleges and universities
    community colleges, 87–89
    competition, 5
    costs of, 73
    faculty salaries, 42
    graduates, 1, 53
    location and proximity, 107, 121
    public and private, 58–59, 64–65
    rate of return, 47, 48, 50, 73
    revenues, 82
    spending by, 13
    standard setting by, 44
    tax credits and deductions, 2–4
    two-year, 6, 43, 47 n 6, 61, 64–65, 110
    wage premium, 2, 53–55
    See also Education, postsecondary; Enrollment; Tuition
Costs of education
    effects on enrollment, 63 n 9
    forgone earnings, 5–7
    out-of-pocket, 5–6, 7
    postsecondary, 56–59
    primary-secondary, 43
    public and private institutions, 58–59
    tuition and, 58
    variation in, 60–61

Demographic issues, 59, 72, 73
Department of Education, 69

Economic issues
    educational level, 1, 9–10, 15, 38–39, 41, 47, 53, 72, 77
    family income, 54–55
    funds transfers, 6, 20, 21, 22, 68
    human capital, 26, 50, 83
    means-based tuition subsidies, 46
    means testing, 57
    national growth rate and human capital, 9–10, 22
    national tuition policy, 116–17
    public debate on federal policies, 4
    rate of return on education, 47, 48, 50, 73, 76, 77, 87, 89
    standard of living, 1
    tax deduction of interest, 49–50
    tuition and financial aid policies, 76–118
    wage differentials, 1, 17, 20, 53–55, 76, 79–81, 116, 118
    See also Labor issues; Tax issues
Education
    educational attainment, 85, 95
    educational level of work force, 1, 41
    effects of market structure on performance, 39, 41, 50–51
    federal budget issues, 28, 29–31, 44–51
    government involvement in, 10–11
    improvement of, 73
    incentives, 22, 24–25
    as an investment, 9–10
    life-cycle analysis, 95–105, 114, 118

payoff of, 7
public and private, 12, 20
reform proposals, 69–72
spending per student, 11
standard years of education, 22, 41
student investment in, 36–38
vouchers, 24–25
See also Schools
Education Individual Retirement Accounts (EIRAs). *See* Individual Retirement Accounts
Education, postsecondary
compared with primary-secondary education, 28–38
competition, 5, 23, 29–35, 38–39, 42–43, 48
cost of, 57–58
effects of tax changes, 66–69
as an entitlement, 44
federal budget issues, 28–31, 44–50
financial assistance to students, 3–4, 23, 25, 26, 43
foreign students, 17, 41–42
funding for, 29–36
incentives for improvement, 19–20
as an investment, 5, 9, 39
issues, 4, 8–9
national policies, 2–4, 6
problems, 5
productivity, 41–42
public and private, 6, 58–59, 64
quality and performance, 17–19, 20, 26
rate of return, 47, 48, 50, 73
reforming public subsidies for, 53–72
remedial role, 5, 22, 43–44, 47
spending by, 13
student investment in, 36–38, 44–45
See also Colleges and universities; Enrollment
Education, primary-secondary
class size, 19, 26
compared with postsecondary education, 28–38
competition, 5, 15–17, 29–36, 38–40, 43, 44

costs of, 42
as entitlement, 39
federal budget issues, 28–31, 50
financial assistance and funding, 25–26, 29–31, 33–34, 43
human capital investment, 11–13
incentives for improvement, 19, 21, 50
issues, 4
problems, 5, 13, 21–22
productivity, 41–42
public policies, 19
quality and performance, 13–14, 15–17, 19, 21, 25–26, 42, 43
unions, 22
See also Schools
EIRAs (Education Individual Retirement Accounts). *See* Individual Retirement Accounts
Enrollment
college costs and tuition, 58–66, 87–89, 109–17
earnings differential and, 53–55
effects of family background, 100–109
effects of family income, 53–55, 83–116
effects of financial aid, 6, 7, 26, 117–18
effects on income, 2
increase in, 5
labor markets and, 73, 107
Ethnic and minority issues
college enrollment gap, 81–82, 90–95, 110–14, 118, 120–21
educational attainment, 77–79, 83, 95–110, 120–21
effects of tuition, 110–12
family background, 95–110, 120
family incomes, 81–82, 92–95
high school certification and graduation, 84, 90–94, 98, 99, 100–105, 118
Pell grants, 121
performance gap, 17
test scores, 18, 25
tuition charges, 121

Family issues
ability to pay tuition and costs, 57–59, 63, 69, 78, 83–83, 89–95

awareness of grant programs, 66, 69, 114
contribution toward college costs, 88
effects on college enrollment, 6, 59–61, 63, 77, 100–109
effects of family income, 54–55, 57–58, 78, 81–82, 89–94, 98–116, 118
ethnic groups, 93–110, 120
family background or environment, 60, 77–78, 84–87, 93–110, 114–16, 118
Individual Retirement Accounts, 48
school choice, 39
See also Armed Forces Qualification Test
Financial aid, student
abuse of, 70–71
application process, 71–72
criticism of, 56
current approach to, 55–58
economic factors, 76–77, 81–82
effects of, 23, 79–81
eligibility for, 56–57, 71, 88, 114
federal proposals in 1997, 3–4, 6, 66–67
loans, 67, 71, 88
low-income students, 6, 23
means testing, 56–57, 71–72
middle-class students, 6
need for, 3
needs-based, 20
prepaid tuition plans, 67
reforms for public subsidies, 53–74
student loans, 49–50, 56, 67
subsidized, 71, 82
total disbursements, 82 n 9
See also Grants; Hope tax credit; Pell grants; Tax credit for lifelong learning

G-7 countries, 15–17, 41
General education diploma (GED), 91, 101–2. See also Schools
GI Bill, 3
Goals 2000, 10–11
Government, 9–10, 55–56
Government, federal

human capital policy, 26
role in education, 13, 20, 23–27, 42–44, 50–51
school finance, 29–34, 71, 82–83
student loans, 56
Government, state and local
grant programs, 56, 58, 61–63
investment in human capital, 13
school finance, 20, 29–34, 55–56, 58, 72, 82
Grants, 6, 56, 65, 82–83. See also Financial aid; Pell grants

Higher Education Act reauthorization (1992), 57
High school. See Schools
High School and Beyond Survey (1982), 61
Hispanics. See Ethnic and minority issues
Hope tax credit, 4, 29, 30, 31, 44–45, 46–47, 66, 78, 81, 117, 118

Income. See Economic issues; Family issues
Individual Retirement Accounts (IRAs), 4, 29, 30, 31, 45–46, 48–49, 66, 68

Job Training Partnership Act, 114

K–12 education. See Education, primary-secondary; Schools

Labor issues, 22, 35, 79–81, 107, 120–21. See also Economic issues
Legal issues, 41
Lifelong learning tax credit. See Tax credit for lifelong learning
Low-income students. See Students, low-income

Making Schools Work: Improving Performance and Controlling Costs (Brookings Institution), 22
Minnesota, 43–44, 51

National Assessment of Educational Progress (NAEP), 15, 17, 25
National Commission on the Cost of Higher Education (1998), 2 n 2, 58

National Governors' Conference (1989), 17
National Longitudinal Survey of Youth (NLSY), 90
National Postsecondary Student Aid Survey (1992), 43
NLSY. *See* National Longitudinal Survey of Youth

Panel Study of Income Dynamics, 114, 115
PCHE. *See* President's Commission on Higher Education
Pell grants, 25, 45
    budget (1998), 29, 30, 31, 45–46
    distributions of, 56, 88
    effects of, 6, 45–46, 63, 64, 65, 66, 70, 78, 113–14
    ethnic and minority groups, 121
    fungibility, 38
    increases (1997), 4
    knowledge and use of, 65, 89, 113–14
    reform proposals, 69–71
Perkins loans. *See* Financial aid
Plus loans. *See* Financial aid
Policies and policy making
    educational, 8, 13, 20, 23, 26, 83, 118
    issues for public discussion, 4–5, 8–9
    role of federal government, 23–24
    tuition, 116–17
    wage subsidies, 76–77
Political issues, 2, 21, 23, 27
Population. *See* Demographic issues
President's Commission on Higher Education (PCHE 1947), 3

Racial issues. *See* Ethnic and minority issues
Reagan, Ronald, 10
Research
    educational, 23–24, 26–27, 60–65, 73–74
    effects of family income, 89
    problems with Current Populations Survey (CPS) data, 119–20
    social experimentation programs, 24

Schools
    Catholic, 36
    charter, 25, 29, 30, 31
    class size, 19, 26
    competition, 38–39
    construction funding, 29, 31
    effects of market structure on performance, 38–41
    finance and funding, 29–35
    high school attendance, certification, and graduation, 84–87, 90–92, 96–98, 99, 100–10, 115–16, 118
    private versus public, 35–36, 39, 40
    school districts, 31–32
    See also Education
Social issues, 77
Stafford loans. *See* Financial aid
Student loans. *See* Financial aid
Students, 56, 71
Students, low-income
    college enrollment, 54–55, 61, 62–65, 66, 81, 84, 87, 89
    effects of tuition, 111–12
    financial aid, 6, 23, 65–66, 87–88
    Pell grants, 63, 89
Subsidies. *See* Financial aid

Tax credit for lifelong learning (TCLL), 4, 29, 30, 31, 45, 48, 66
Tax issues
    capital gains, 67
    effects of, 20, 69, 84
    local school finance, 33–34
    means testing, 56–57
    national tuition policy, 116–17
    state taxes, 56
    targeting, 67–68
    tax credits, 2–4, 21, 26, 27, 29, 31, 45, 48, 50, 66–67, 117
    tax deductions, 29, 30, 49–50, 67, 72, 84
    See also Economic issues
Taxpayer Relief Act of 1997, 2–4
TCLL. *See* Tax credit for lifelong learning
Teachers, 12, 13, 25, 42. *See also* Labor issues
Technology Literacy Challenge Fund, 29, 30, 31

Testing, 13–15, 18, 19, 25
Third International Math and Science Study (TIMSS), 15
Title I, 25–26, 29, 30, 31
Tuition
    effects on enrollment, 60–61, 65, 87–89, 109–14, 117
    effects on high school graduation rates, 107 n 29
    effects of Hope tax credit on, 47–48
    effects of increased enrollments, 58
    effects of Pell grants on, 46
    effects of tax changes, 47, 68–69
    effects on wage inequality, 117, 118
    ethnic and minority groups, 121
    expansion of high-skilled worker supply, 80–81
    federal support for, 3–4
    increases in, 2, 6, 20, 58–59, 82, 83 n 10
    national policies, 116–17
    problems in paying, 2, 3
    public and private institutions, 58–59
    regulation of, 20–21
    relationship to costs of education, 20, 58
    See also Costs; Family issues; Pell grants

Unions. See Labor issues
United States, 11, 13–15, 17

Vouchers. See Education

Work-study programs, 31, 88